THE CROSSED HANDS OF GOD

THE CROSSED HANDS OF GOD

The World War I Diary and Letters of
Eugene William McLaurin

Edited By
Jerry R. Tompkins

Foreword By
Jay Winter

RESOURCE *Publications* · Eugene, Oregon

THE CROSSED HANDS OF GOD
The World War I Diary and Letters of Eugene William McLaurin

Resource Publications
An Imprint of Wipf and Stock Publishers
199 W. 8th Ave., Suite 3
Eugene, OR 97401

www.wipfandstock.com

ISBN 13: 978-1-4982-2137-5

Manufactured in the U.S.A.   08/31/2015

To
Marcia...

and in memory
of
our parents

who lived in the time
of
The Great War

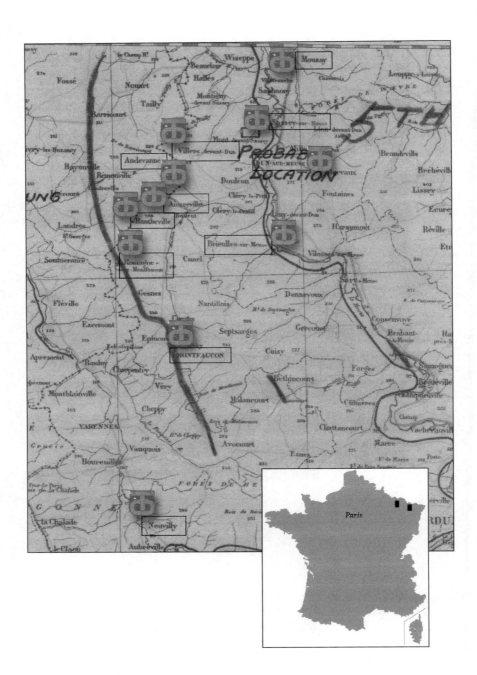

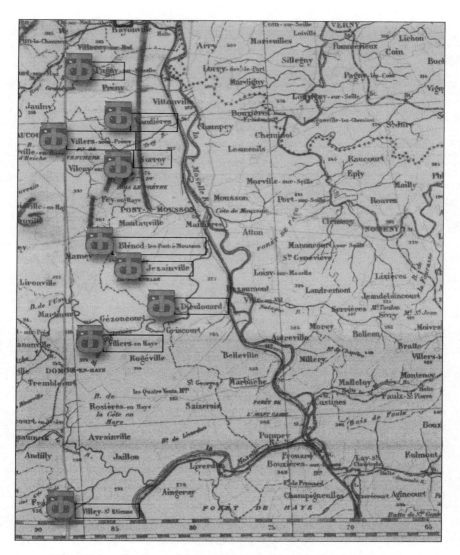

Although the offensives are historically distinct (St. Mihiel, right, September 12–16, and Meuse-Argonne, left, September 26-October 1), McLaurin's movements, as reflected in the diary, indicate that he was ordered back and forth between the two areas for burial detail. The outline map shows the location of the battle zones east of Paris.

Contents

Foreword

THIS SET OF DOCUMENTS describes facets of the First World War rarely addressed in American historical narratives. It covers the American involvement both in the fighting in northern France in the last five months of the war and as an occupying force in Germany in 1919. Like other collections of the personal papers of American soldiers of the Great War which families have preserved and published, it shows both the naiveté and the sophistication of those Americans thrown into the war in its last phase.

While Eugene William McLaurin endured five months of war, the French and British soldiers "associated" with the American army endured fifty months of combat. I say "associated" because the term "Allied" was insufficiently independent for many back at home. The relatively short American encounter with war explains McLaurin's initial *sangfroid* about artillery, his sense that the German army fought "unfairly" by seizing every possible topographical advantage, and his absence of any doubt about the outcome of the war. Soldiers with a longer experience of this, the first war between all the great industrialized nations, knew better.

McLaurin's diary and letters are unusual in that he was not an infantryman but a stretcher-bearer assigned to burial details. These moved to wherever the bodies were. He had hoped to secure a commission as a chaplain, but Army red tape delayed a decision until the war was over; then the Army was no longer commissioning chaplains. McLaurin served as a private soldier, who moved across and through different theaters a bit like Pierre in Tolstoy's *War and Peace*. He was at the war but did not see combat. What he did see was the human wreckage of war, and he provided a dignified burial to dead soldiers wherever that was possible.

The mix of domestic and military detail in these documents describes the world of all the 70 million soldiers who put on a uniform during the Great War. In effect, between 1914 and 1918, family history and the history of war intersected, and they have never been fully separated since. The crossed hands of war arose out of its democratization, and millions of young men bore its traces until their dying days. In McLaurin's case, that was until 1978.

Throughout the world, in countless attics, garages, and storerooms, there are diaries, letters, and photographs of soldiers of the Great War. They are appearing in great numbers now, a century after the outbreak of the 1914–18 conflict, and all are to be welcomed. They enable us to glimpse the moment when the scourge of industrialized warfare on a global scale came to the world.

Soldiers fought for their country, but they also fought for their families, or in this case, the families they would have when they returned home. His fiancée and their future together grounded McLaurin, and provided him with a powerful sense that his time at war was a step on the way to a long and rich Christian life.

More than 100,000 Americans were not so fortunate. For too many years, the screen memory of the Second World War has occluded the story of American service and sacrifice in the First World War. Twice as many Americans died in active service in the First World War than died in the Vietnam conflict. Their voices and those of their surviving comrades deserve to be heard, and for that, we owe the editors of this body of evidence our thanks and our respect.

Jay Winter

The Charles J. Stille Professor of History,
Yale University

Preface

LIKE MANY ITEMS FAMILIES keep in closets and attics—items which move with the family to new homes only to be placed in yet another closet or attic, Eugene McLaurin's World War I diary and letters to his fiancée were saved, kept in boxes, and moved around Texas, from Edna to Sweetwater to Ballinger to Houston to Austin and finally, as Eugene and Myrtle McLaurin retired, to their two successive houses occupied during their years in Waskom, Texas, from 1958–1971.

As Myrtle's health declined, nursing care needs led to the couple's move to Presbyterian Village in Dallas. Downsizing involved turning over many things—including the World War I diary and the letters—to their only son and heir, Lock McLaurin, then living in Houston.

Still again, the diary and letters travelled from Houston to the suburb of Pearland and thence to Katy, Texas.

Lock was a good steward of his father's World War I memorabilia. In time, he gave the original diary to a daughter who carefully stored it in a box in her attic, but he held on to other items.

It was not until 2011, when I became serious about publishing the diary and some of the letters, that Lock drew the diary and the letters from their repositories and provided me with useful excerpts and commentary as well as copies of some of the letters.

The letters, like the diary, reveal a man who possessed a deep awareness and observation of people and places, as well as respectable writing and composition skills. While the diary was intensely focused on the events of combat, often as a good reporter would record them, the letters are more revealing of the evolving inner man. This is a man who survived the terror of combat but was soon thrust into what most soldiers remember following combat: homesickness, boredom, and the first phase of reflecting on the awfulness of recent events in order to discover meanings that will bind his experience and lead to a deeper understanding of his own life as well as to a vision of a renewed future.

Jerry Tompkins

April 6, 2015

Acknowledgments

LAUCHLIN ARTHUR McLAURIN, the only son of Eugene McLaurin and Myrtle Arthur McLaurin, is known among family and friends as "Lock." During a visit in 2002 he mentioned that his father, a veteran of World War I, had kept a diary. He lent me a typed copy. Later I learned that Lock was, and is now, the steward of a remarkable collection of World War I artifacts which had belonged to his father. His granting me access to the diary as well as to the entire collection made this volume possible.

DAVID F. BEER is a university professor of technical communication whose avocation has been the study of World War I. A published author, I asked him to read the McLaurin diary. He soon came back with suggestions for expanding the scope of plans for possible publication and made especially helpful suggestions regarding the McLaurin biographical section.

JAMES STUART CURRIE was the first to read a draft of the comprehensive collection of materials that would become *The Crossed Hands of God*, and he offered effective guidance in my search for a suitable publisher. A friend and respected colleague, he deserves my profound gratitude.

RANDAL WHITTINGTON read the manuscript and was my consultant in all aspects of the project. Nonchalantly creative, she met deadlines with ease. Her work and the cheerfulness with which she accomplished it will be long remembered and appreciated.

LILLY CARREL undertook the daunting task of scanning and transcribing McLaurin's letters to his fiancee, Myrtle Arthur. The stationery is almost a century old and McLaurin's handwriting not always easy to decipher, but she demonstrated a consistent professionalism throughout the project.

KRISTY SORENSEN, archivist, made useful suggestions regarding the handling of fragile memorabilia and artifacts and has provided secure storage for various McLaurin materials.

CLAUDIE PELTS HUDSON, a Parisian by birth, knows the landscape of her native France. She used her mapping skills to identify and label some two dozen locations, several obscure and elusive, which form the personal map of McLaurin's World War I journey.

Illustrations and Photographs

Map: Library of Congress Geography and Map Division, Charles Pelot Summerall map collection, map showing position of German Army geologic stations, St. Mihiel sector. [1918?]; Scale 1:200,000. 1 map : ms., col.; on sheet 53 x 95 cm., G5834.S3418C5 1918 .M3

"Camp Travis from wireless, Fort Sam Houston, Texas, 1917," Library of Congress Prints and Photographs Division, LC-USZ62-134757, 1 gelatin silver print; 9 x 60 in.

"Removing the dead from the trenches [World War I]," Library of Congress Prints and Photographs Division, photographic print on stereo card, c1919 Sept. 18.

"90th Division bakery at Berncastle, Germany," World War I Signal Corps photograph collection, U.S. Army Heritage and Education Center, taken 1919 January 29.

The Edna Herald, June 26, 1919 A post-war tribute from McLaurin's commanding officer-chaplain

New Town Cemetery, Elysian Fields, Texas, Photo by Heather McPherson

All other photographs used in this book are from McLaurin's personal collection with his own captions.

Introduction

THOUGH ONE OF THOUSANDS of diaries during World War I, the one kept by Eugene William McLaurin for sixty-five days offers a fresh view of that hell in which hundreds of thousands lived and died in the St. Mihiel and Meuse-Argonne drives that culminated in an armistice on November 11, 1918. For one thing, McLaurin was almost thirty years of age and, for another, he was an ordained minister who was exempt from being drafted. He did not tell us why he volunteered. I probe that unanswered question in the sketch which will follow shortly, but the hypotheses are mine, not his.

His writing style is reportorial. McLaurin spends no time reflecting on missing home and very little on the senselessness of the war. While he becomes acquainted with danger on every hand, he is not preoccupied with thoughts of death. He does not pretend to be a poet or historian, but his sense of fulfilling his duty appears again and again in non-egotistical ways, leaving the reader with the notion that he was, simply and consistently, a brave man.

The inclusion of letters from McLaurin to his fiancée, Myrtle Alice Arthur, a young woman in his congregation, was a late decision. The hesitation was due to the nature of the letters themselves. They were clearly intended to be personal and confidential. In content they are essentially love letters, infused with a yearning created by indefinite separation, but filled with news and observations by a rather provincial Southerner experiencing a larger world. They are romantic and passionate, though consistently held within the bounds of a Victorian decorum. Ultimately I came to believe the letters could not be left out. In them we find the wholeness of the man. The diary reveals a man of dependable courage but with little self-consciousness that he was being anything but faithful to his calling. The letters reveal the heart of the man, the corporal expression of a self bound by flesh and blood, but filled with a diffused sense of purpose and dedication to everything he believes in. One thing he believes in with all his heart is Myrtle Arthur.

Finally, there can be no biography apart from context, a place. For McLaurin that place, that beginning point, was 19th-century rural Mississippi.

The Life of Eugene William McLaurin

By Jerry R. Tompkins

Heritage: His Family, Faith, and Education

AUGUST IS A WEARY month in the lower South, a time when rainfall wanes and the earth turns brown and leaves begin to drop as though autumn had already arrived. The sunlight itself is different in August, especially if a brief unexpected shower occurs. Toward evening, the air turns to an amber hue and the world seems to hang listless and spent.

Margaret Rachael Mathison McLaurin was as weary as the land and was glad when her time came to deliver her first son, Eugene William McLaurin, born August 21, 1888. There would be three more sons before a daughter would arrive, then another son, and finally two more daughters—eight in all.

The father, Hugh Calhoun McLaurin, was fourth generation out of Scotland and third generation to live in Simpson County, Mississippi. The McLaurins had come to Simpson County from what is now Scotland County, North Carolina. Two generations before, this particular branch of McLaurins had migrated to the United States from the Port Appin area of Argyll, Scotland.

Although the Mathisons had begun their American odyssey from the Isle of Jura just off the west coast of Scotland, it is believed that the McLaurin and Mathison families had known one another even back in Scotland, and most certainly in the United States before their arrivals in Mississippi in about 1821.

The promise of more fertile land in Mississippi, where the land had been renewed by eons of frequent and vast flooding from the Mississippi River and its tributaries, drew settlers from the Carolinas where land prices were inflated.

Often settlers would migrate in groups, having bought land adjacent to, or at least in proximity to, their former, now continuing, neighbors. Among those of Scottish heritage new to an area, a Presbyterian church would soon be organized. Occasionally, the Presbyterian minister and his family accompanied the settlers. In any case, a church was soon established in the area west of Mt. Olive. A congregation had been founded in 1830. It was called the Hopewell Presbyterian Church.

The first church building was a one-room affair which also served as a school. The very existence of the school is worthy of note. Flung down on corners of obscure farms across the state were dozens of one-room schools, taught by marginally prepared teachers for a few months a year and attended by farm children who rode horses or mules or walked over sometimes muddy, virtually impassible roads to catch a few weeks of schooling punctuated by planting, picking cotton, harvesting, and other farm chores. This reduced education to a sparse, hit-or-miss venture on the part of everyone touched by its sketchy promise and meager delivery.

By 1885, three years before Eugene McLaurin was born, the Mississippi Legislature had adopted a law requiring that children attend a state-approved school for at least four months a year. The law was widely ignored. To provide such schools required taxes, and Mississippians were among the poorest in the nation, as they are to this day. There were the hard realities about the necessities of life, and education was not high on the list.

Still, for Presbyterians, education was of fundamental and compelling value. Something deep in their Scottish psyche was lodged the notion that one's work, whether or not it was of worldly sophistication, required a preparation of the mind, and that required a commitment on the part of both a teacher and a pupil to submit to the discipline of learning, however simple and inadequate that endeavor might be.

With his devout family, Eugene McLaurin faithfully attended worship at the Hopewell Church. Between Sundays he worked on the family farm. It is not clear what his earliest educational opportunities were.

All this was being lived out in a certain lingering societal context. One remembers that when Eugene McLaurin was born, the Civil War was a recent memory, its inexhaustible misery still abroad in all of Mississippi. Blacks, recently freed, usually remained in the area which had been their home in bondage. Their numbers often exceeded that of whites. The poor of both races needed work and often competed for work that paid little to members of either race, but always less to blacks. The pervasive

sense of defeat and hopelessness provided the motivation to remain isolated and defensive.

When Eugene McLaurin was born, Jefferson Davis, the only president of the Confederate States of America, was still living, and continuing to write his painstaking memoirs at Beauvoir near Biloxi. And thirty
miles east of the McLaurin farm was Jones County, remembered by many
as the Free State of Jones, virtually the only county in the South to secede
from the Confederacy, which gave the immediate region a strong sense of
isolation and disconnection.

By the late 1890s, Eugene McLaurin was demonstrating that he was
a highly motivated student. At some point, he began attending school
at Oak Vale, a community some forty miles southwest of the McLaurin
farm. It can be assumed that he roomed and boarded in the Oak Vale
community, perhaps in the home of a kinsman. He next entered high
school at Mt. Olive in Covington County, approximately eight miles from
the McLaurin farm. The distance was too great for McLaurin to walk;
perhaps he rode a horse to school.

In 1907, he graduated from Mt. Olive High School and that fall enrolled in the University of Mississippi at Oxford, fondly known then and
now as "Ole Miss." He proved capable of not only performing well as a
student, he also joined the football squad, then coached by Frank Mason.
Mason was among the first coaches who would help make football into
the iconic, trademark collegial sport it is today, often eclipsing the superior academic status of outstanding universities.

McLaurin left Ole Miss at the end of his freshman year, transferring
to Southwestern Presbyterian University at Clarksville, Tennessee. He continued his academic pursuits and his football activity, for which he received
more than a little notice playing right end on the Southwestern team.

Meanwhile, the McLaurin family had decided to relocate from Mississippi to Tom Green County in West Texas where cotton farming had
become a more profitable endeavor. But in less than two years, the family
realized its move had been a mistake. Somehow, in spite of cheap land
and a more promising future, the McLaurins found the environment
to be alien to their sense of place and home, so Hugh McLaurin again
sold out and moved back in the direction of a more hospitable, familiar
environment.

After two years at Southwestern, McLaurin dropped out of college
for a year, probably in order to help his family make its move from West
Texas to East Texas and the picturesque little town of Elysian Fields.

But before beginning the move from the San Angelo area, McLaurin and two of his brothers took temporary jobs with a railroad company. They laid track for a new rail route which would ultimately run from San Angelo to Ft. Stockton and Presidio, thence across northern Mexico and ultimately to the Gulf of California. The work was backbreaking and the West Texas sun unmerciful, but it paid well. Traveling back home to San Angelo by train was possible only twice a week, and once the McLaurin brothers decided to walk back, beginning just east of El Dorado, mostly at night to avoid the intense heat. The distance was about forty miles. Years later Eugene would remember walking with head down and eyes fixed on the road bed where rattlesnakes waited to attack anything that moved, especially a hapless railroad worker.

The work was physically enhancing to McLaurin, who was by now aware of his exceptional skill at football. The following year, when he returned to Southwestern for his senior year, he would even take up boxing as a training method for quickening his movements on the football field. At the end of the 1911–12 academic year, McLaurin received his bachelor of arts degree. Although the record is now lost, it is believed that he was also nominated as an All-American football player. Whether that is accurate or not, McLaurin's splendid physical development was obvious. Even in his 80s, his family and friends would note his fine, confident posture and his still-substantial shoulders. He continued to walk vigorously on a daily regimen until shortly before his death.

**Working on the railroad, San Angelo to El Dorado, 1910;
McLaurin third from right**

**McLaurin's first pastorate was Allen Memorial
Presbyterian Church in Edna, Texas**

The University, Seminary, and Early Ministry

Beyond the early years of faithful attendance in worship at Hopewell
Church, we know nothing of the process of spiritual discernment which
led him to a sense of a calling to the gospel ministry. What we do know
is that McLaurin chose Austin Presbyterian Theological Seminary as the
place where he would receive his training as a future pastor. He refused
to be less than fully occupied, so he enrolled simultaneously in the University of Texas. In 1916, in virtually back-to-back commencements, he
was awarded a bachelor of divinity degree from Austin Seminary and a
master of arts degree from the University of Texas.

Now qualified and available to seek a pastorate, McLaurin accepted a
call to the Allen Memorial Presbyterian Church in Edna, Texas, a county
seat community of under 5000 in a town well located between Houston
and Victoria. The congregation was in the 200- to 300-member range,
ideal for a man in his first pastorate—large enough to be stable, small
enough to enable a minister to provide pastoral care for all its members.
Among those members was a young woman, Myrtle Arthur. It would be
another six years, but in 1922 she became McLaurin's wife.

When McLaurin was ordained in September 1916, the war in Europe had been underway for more than two years, its horrors rising to a
new crescendo in the spring and summer of 1915. In 1916 came Verdun

with casualties numbering a million more or less and fought along a battle line which, when the carnage eased briefly, remained unchanged. Then there was the Somme.

Still, the US remained aloof, reinforced by President Woodrow Wilson's pledge to keep the nation out of Europe's terrible ordeal. But the president changed his mind, and on April 2, 1917, he asked Congress to declare war on Germany.

Nationwide recruitment proved easier than anyone dreamed. Songs, silent movies, and stunningly beautiful poster art captivated the hearts of countless American men—and women, too—and soon a nation which had not known a real war in fifty years was ready to fight "over there."

It was not long until the impact of "over there" became "over here." Like young men across the country, the boys of Edna, Texas, were joining up. Most would find themselves training in San Antonio in the army's 90th Division of the American Expeditionary Forces, a division made up largely of men from Texas and Oklahoma.

In April 1918, the gentle pastor of Allen Memorial Presbyterian Church volunteered for army duty as a chaplain and was immediately sent to Camp Travis in San Antonio for his basic training. He had expected to receive a commission. He never did, and he ended up serving his entire time in the army as a private.

One can ask why a man approaching thirty years of age would sign on to endure the physical demands of basic training and the risks of being wounded—maimed—or killed. Perhaps the question is answered in the question itself. Time was moving him toward the middle years, and the risks themselves offered challenges. Or perhaps he was caught up in the excitement of younger men joining up and shipping out. Perhaps it was an uncomplicated patriotism. And though it may have been unlikely, perhaps this son of the South wanted to demonstrate a refutation of the often-expressed doubts about the loyalty of recruits from the South. After all, Appomattox was barely fifty years in the past. Folks as young as sixty could remember the conflict and its bitter aftermath. But that was, for America's younger generation, in the past.

His War Diary: Duty, Destruction, and Death

Thus the Reverend Eugene McLaurin in 1918 found himself serving as a private in the AEF in France with a 90th Division Supply Train. In September of that year he was suddenly sought out by the divisional chaplain to become a non-commissioned temporary chaplain for the 360th Infantry. At this time, on September 9, Eugene McLaurin also began a diary which gives us a unique view of the final months of the war through the eyes of an acting padre. His training for the job was brief, as his diary entry for September 11 records:

> Chaplain Reese was at Headquarters with two motorcycles and side-cars. Threw my pack in. Chaplain Reese called me inside and told me the attack on the German lines was to begin that night. We had been expecting it for some time. At the same time, in less than one minute, he gave me complete instructions and training in what I was to do, shoved about fifty grave markers into my hand, and told me to get into one side-car while he got in the other.

And off he went. The American push into the St. Mihiel salient was about to begin, and McLaurin's duties, it turned out, would primarily be to identify and bury the dead.

Until 2003, McLaurin's neatly hand-written diary lay in obscurity in his son's and later his granddaughter's homes, treasured by his family along with his uniform, medals, and several letters. At some point after the war the diary was typed up, a version which comes to some thirty pages of print covering from September 9, 1918, to the last day of the war, November 11, where it ends.

The diary provides not only a vivid picture of Private McLaurin's war experiences, but also of his character and ability to observe and record details of the happenings around him in a direct and honest way. As with most soldiers in combat, he is not interested in the "big picture" of grand movements and strategies or of political maneuvers and international diplomatic ploys, but in the right here and now. Today is all that can matter. Entries vary from a sentence (October 14: "I managed for new clothes today,") to by far the longest and most detailed entry of several pages for November 1, beginning "This has been a long and a terrible day," marking the start of the American advance between the Aisne and Meuse Rivers in the Argonne Forest.

Camp Travis, San Antonio, Texas

ENLISTMENT RECORD.

Name: *Eugene W. McLaurin*   Grade: *Private*

Enlisted *Apr. 26* , 191 *8* , at *Edna, Texas*

Serving in *first* _____ enlistment period at date of discharge.

Prior service:* *None*

Noncommissioned officer: *Never*

Marksmanship, gunner qualification or rating: *None*

Horsemanship: *Not mounted*

Battles, engagements, skirmishes, expeditions: *A.E.F. Left U.S. Sept. Air France 9/18 Left France 9/8/19 Oct. 21 9/19 Villers en Haye Sector - St. Mihiel Offensive Puvenelle Sector - Meuse Argonne Offensive - Army of Occupation*

Knowledge of any vocation: *Ministering*

Wounds received in service: *None*

Physical condition when discharged: *Good*

Typhoid prophylaxis completed *9/8/19*

Paratyphoid prophylaxis completed *9/8/19*

Married or single: *Single*

Character: *Excellent*

Remarks: *No A.W.O.L. absence under G.O.# or no. as noted. Member of 65th Co. 165th D.B. Co. B 315th Supply Train Hqrs. Co. 360th Inf.*

Signature of soldier: *Eugene W. McLaurin*

O. E. ____
Captain ____
Commanding *____*

* Give company and regiment or corps or department, with inclusive dates of service in each enlistment.
† Give date of qualification or rating and number, date, and source of order announcing same.

Many entries are uncompromisingly blunt, depicting events that could hardly be described in a letter home that would pass through the censors, such as this early entry:

> *I slept in trench with runner. I buried Clarence H. Braschel, and parts of an unidentified body. Only one leg and the head could be found. The head had been blown up into a tree, 40 feet away.*

On September 21 he confesses that he never was so tired in all his life. Thus the diary gives us insights into a world of discomfort, fear, and horror experienced by the fighting soldiers on the front line, all presented in an almost matter-of-fact manner with no attempts to either embellish or understate. Above all, McLaurin is focused on doing the best he can in the world of war.

This world is primarily one of rain, mud, and death. Mud and rain permeate life at the front and even far behind the lines. On September 11, the third day of the diary, McLaurin "Slept in a truck. Cold and wet." Later that day he takes his grave markers some seven kilometers, as ordered, while it "Rained on us all the way—lots of mud and water." Several days later a trip to meet a graves-registration man is "one of the muddiest I have ever made," and by October 11, after a march back to the rear, he fears that his "tendons of Achilles have about broken in two. I think it is caused by having so much mud to walk through. The mud is everywhere, even on the paved highways." While marching through Avocourt, "of which not a single wall remained standing," the mud makes marching slow and tiresome, and even the entry for the last day of the war, November 11, records that the streets on the way to Division Headquarters at Mouzay were "several inches deep in mud and slush." Perhaps a short observation in the fairly lengthy entry for October 16 sums up the constant underfoot conditions: "The roads were muddy as usual."

Besides foul weather, the skies carry deadlier hazards for McLaurin and his comrades. The decimating violence of shells and shrapnel, as well as the insidious possibility of poisonous gas, made life at the front tenuous. His entry for September 15, beginning simply with, "This has been a full day," continues to describe how as the battalion advanced.

> *Shells began to fall. Before, they had come only intermittently. But now about 11 o'clock, a.m., as the 2nd Bn. came across, they came like hail. As I was up on the hillside, some distance, I had a view of the whole Bn. as it came down the hillside. Although the Germans threw a box barrage around them, they came on, never faltering,*

never turning back, or even looking toward the rear. By this time,
I was in a shell hole, as the shrapnel had begun falling too close.
Contrary to my previous ideas, only a very few men were being
hit. The shelling increased in violence as the advance came to the
foot of the slope. The noise was terrific.

The next day gas shells ruin their food supplies and force the men to put on their masks. The day's entry concludes with:

Several shells fell as I left town, and I ran into a strong concen-
tration of mustard gas. I had to put on my gas mask, and I was
entirely out of breath when I reached the pill-box. This is one time
I did without supper.

Two days later McLaurin is in Vandieres to bury two victims of shelling. The bodies were in an advanced stage of decomposition. Both men had evidently been killed in the drive Sunday morning. They had taken cover in a sunken road, and two shells landed near them, one in the soft dirt of a vineyard, and the other on a rocky surface. It was the latter shell that killed them.

Later, on October 27, he and another chaplain hold five services for the men, during which shells fall around them. He is gradually becoming inured, however, for on the 28th he writes:

The shelling last night was rather severe and prolonged; several of
the boys moved into a shallow, broad ditch. I did not move, but
slept through most of the shelling. Occasionally a loud one would
wake me. Some of those big ones must have come from a long
distance. It is remarkable how safe one feels when shells are falling
with only the frailest covering for a protection. I had only my pup-
tent, but I felt reasonably safe. After each explosion I would turn
over and go to sleep again.

Yet events never allow him to become nonchalant about danger. More than once he sees several men wounded by shells, and one day shelling is so intense that no one will go out on a burying detail with him. Burial detail was one of the acting chaplain's primary duties, and he quickly becomes no stranger to the victims of bullets and shrapnel. The actual digging of graves was not, strictly speaking, his responsibility, but he is always willing to lend a hand. Burying soldiers during warfare carries its own hazards: on September 19 he takes German prisoners to assist him with the burials and the following day he has to wait until dark to perform some burials "on account of the bodies being in direct observation of the enemy's balloons." But it is the "terrible day" of October 5, when the Germans shell the P.C. (Post of Command) all day long and McLaurin and others take refuge in the dug-out, that we get a more detailed description of his life at the front and the inevitable emotions that result.

> *Several times shells hit near the P.C., and one time the violence of the concussion forced open a heavy door. With each explosion a distinct tremor could be felt in the earth. No one was wounded, however, until about dusk; then a big H.E. [high explosive] landed on "B" Company's P.C. and caved in one room. In this room at the time were three or four men. Drohan and Conley were killed instantly, and the other escaped injury, but was seriously shell-shocked. Little, a Bn. runner, who was standing in the door from the other room, was blown by the force of the explosion into the other room. He also suffered shell-shock. I went down as soon as it was reported at the P.C. Capt. Hogg was distinctly nervous. Also was everybody else. Already one squad was trying to recover the bodies in hope that life might still be found. Drohan's body was soon recovered from the wreckage. But it was impossible to get Conley's body. With another squad I started digging the graves, where Sgt. Irwin's body was buried. When I came back to the P.C. the litter bearers came up with Drohan's body. He was terribly mangled, the shrapnel having gone into his chest, and warm blood was soaking all over his clothes. I felt horrified when I felt the warm liquid; but I searched every pocket for personal effects, just for the sake of his folks back home. The more I see of this hellish business the more deeply I hate war.*

The following days provided little respite for McLaurin. On October 6, he reports:

> *Tonight, just after dark, we took up front line position, relieving the 2nd Battalion. We passed through "Death Valley" just in time to miss a severe shelling . . . Buried Connely just at daybreak. We did not want Fritz to catch us at work, as he could make it extremely unpleasant. Connely was a Catholic, and his widowed mother's only son. He did not have to come, either; but he insisted on being sent, although he seemed to know something of the coming death. He said all the time that he would never go back.*

With the German army now in retreat, the Americans continue to advance. There is no respite from the fighting and killing in these last days, however, and McLaurin, as his duties require, follows close behind the front. In fact, the last several pages of the diary, from November 1 to the end, make for some of the most compelling and graphic reading in the diary. On November 1 he writes that he has reached the former German front-line positions. All along this front he sees "body after body of German soldiers" and records that:

> Most of them were killed by shell fire—our barrage, but a few of them, I noticed had died from our Infantry. They had stuck by their machine guns until the very last. And in many a machine gun pit was the body of its last defender.

His work continues, as does the horror. He is busier than ever with burial details and with searching for bodies. Many they find have "been dead for some time." On November 4 he records that he and his detail buried eleven Americans and four Germans. On the 5th they sleep on German beds even though "I am sure that we shall all get the cooties." It had been a busy day as usual; one of their tasks had been "to bury a bunch of men out of the 359th, who had been killed almost in the edge of Bantheville. We also buried one German . . . as it was late, we put him into a shell hole and hurriedly threw a little dirt over him." On November 7, just four days before the Armistice of which they have yet to hear, he continues to describe what he sees and must do.

> On the next hill we found one man only the legs from the knees down. Evidently a shell made a direct hit on him. Not another bit of his body could be found. Although shreds of flesh were scattered here and there, already black from decomposition. Fortunately his tags were near, and we were able to establish his identity. He belonged to the 3rd Battalion. And others, also, were torn and horribly mangled. In a terribly shocking manner, they were. One body had the intestine laying [sic] exposed; another had the head split open with a large shell fragment; another had part of his face gone.

By now the work is understandably having its effect on McLaurin and his workmates. On one body he finds a picture of a wife and child, "an infant about six months old." Weariness, bitterness, and anger are finally becoming inevitable, and the entry ends with, "It is another of the glories of war, that it makes widows and orphans." The entry for the 8th is relatively short for these intense days: "We continue our work as usual. It is getting to be very trying to our nerves, and everyone is anxious to be through with this job. It is work that must be done, but no one desires to do it . . . We buried thirty-one Germans today." The next day he records that they feel "shut off from the world, marooned and isolated; we have not been able to get any news in about a week now." They do hear a rumor that Germany has asked for an armistice, yet, as he writes on November 9:

> *We continue our work . . . but so much of our time was spent in searching over a large area that it will take at least another day. Chaplain Lewis says that he has dreamed several nights now about dead men. Last night was my first time. This work is hard on all of us, and I believe eventually it would run a man crazy. Several of the men . . . say that every time they start to eat they think of the dead men . . . and they can't eat.*

McLaurin and his detail work as hard as ever on November 10. He is surprised to find an American body with no visible signs of injury, and he suspects an exploding gas shell was the cause. The whole day is spent searching for bodies, and although they only find two Americans and eight Germans, he estimates they have buried 101 Americans and some seventy Germans on this particular patrol; another chaplain and his detail have buried just about the same number. By now rumors about a ceasefire have reached them, and the men feel hopeful but not yet happy. The last words in his diary the night before the war ends are optimistic but guarded, touched with introspection,

> *German commissioners have actually come across to see Gen. Foch about an armistice. That much at least we now know to be true, even in our isolation. We are fervently praying that it may mean the end; it is too terrible to kill men in such a murderous business. This detail work behind the lines, following up the battle, is even worse. It is enough to drive a man crazy, or to make him absolutely heartless or indifferent about men. God give us peace!*

Peace does come the next day, and McLaurin devotes several pages to what is the final entry of his diary on November 11. Much is covered in these last pages, which understandably open with "At last it is over!" The Armistice had been agreed on at 5 a.m. that morning, and was to take effect officially at 11 a.m. When they learn this, McLaurin records:

> *There was no cheering, or yelling, although there were over fifty of us in the detail. One or two tried to holler, but only a feeble sound was heard. We couldn't say anything that would do justice to the occasion. Our hearts came up into our throats for sheer joy and choked all utterance . . . In spite of the fog, the mud, and the cold,*

*and the long march ahead of us, we were happier than we had
been in many a day.*

Arriving back at Division Headquarters, he and Chaplains Reese
and Lewis "gathered a few officers and men together and held a short
thanksgiving service. There was only one prayer, and a song, 'My Country 'Tis of Thee.' Length is not always essential to earnestness."

Unexpectedly, even though he has done as much as any chaplain
possibly could on the battlefield, McLaurin now learns that a wire has
just been received from G.H.Q. requesting yet another letter of recommendation to make him a full, commissioned chaplain—but "I thought
a commission did not make any difference, now that the war was over."

Further sad absurdity is behind one of his comments in the closing paragraphs of the diary, although McLaurin merely records the fact
without judgment:

> *We had anxiously listened at 11 o'clock to see whether the armi-
> stice was a fake or was really true. At ten minutes until 11 you
> could hear quite a bit of firing, but after 11 not a report was heard.*

The morning of the last day of the war was a busy one. Many on
both sides continued the fight up to the last minute, and thousands lost
their lives. Thus there would still be plenty of work for burial details after
the guns ceased, but McLaurin never reports it. His diary ends with the
fighting, with him in Mouzay, a few miles south of the targeted Stenay.
His final paragraph is almost a paean of thankfulness mingled with faith
and reflection on what he had done and recorded for some two months:

> *Thank God! The war is over—actually, if not formally. No more
> hardship or hunger, or night marches! No more 'going over the top'
> or hiding in 'fox-holes' from the ominous shell or the machine gun
> bullet. No more passing to the rear, walking or on stretchers, either
> mortally wounded, or maimed and disfigured for life. No more
> laying of men wrapped in a blanket in a scooped out shell hole or
> hastily dug grave. Thank God, the terrible destruction of life is at
> last a thing of the past for us! And thank Him again, because vic-
> tory, with the forces of Right and Freedom, and a crushing defeat
> has been administered to militarism. Right is justified once more.*

McLaurin thus completes his diary with a lengthy paean to victory—
exuberant in the exaltation of the hour when it all was at last over. The
emotive quality of the experience was undoubtedly similar to what was
felt and expressed at almost the same moment by millions of American

and European soldiers, but McLaurin had the maturity and the education to write his version with superior expression.

Moreover, the diary reveals that more than once McLaurin broke the cardinal rule for survival among seasoned soldiers of lower rank: never volunteer. But, volunteer he did. He seemed to have had some deep conviction that being idle was a waste of his time and opportunity for service. It would be within the scope of his theology to believe God had placed him there in France at this particular time to offer whatever service was needed which he could provide.

McLaurin was no pacifist, but his anguish in witnessing death even on the German side comes through in numerous and subtle ways. There were events McLaurin does not report. Somewhere along the way, he received at least a whiff of mustard gas, and he suffered some degree of lung distress for years to come. It may account for his move to West Texas for his second pastorate where the air was less humid. Another event is known to us only because it is included in a book entitled *Pastoral Adventure* (New York, 1938) written after the war by McLaurin's supervisor-chaplain, Clarence Herbert Reese, an Episcopal priest. Reese reports, "A shell exploded beside him [McLaurin] once and he wandered about dazed for hours, but refused to go to the rear. When he recovered himself he went on with burying the dead and ministering to the wounded." Chaplain Reese adds, "Since my return, I have had two petitions presented to Congress asking for special legislation granting him the rank and pay of other chaplains, but so far nothing has been done. He served throughout the war with only the rank and pay of a private."

After the Armistice

Following the signing of the Armistice, various units of the army were ordered into Germany for an indefinite period of occupation duty. McLaurin's 315th Supply Train was among them.

In addition to regular chaplain's duties, he reconnected with the YMCA, an organization in which many ordained ministers served in addition to their chaplaincies. This connection was to a great extent due to President Wilson's concern that American soldiers be kept "morally clean." The YMCA provided recreation and entertainment. It built huts, showed movies, hosted civilian and military theatrical groups, provided for athletic contests, and maintained reading and writing rooms. For

McLaurin, these duties came as blessed relief from the horrors of war to which he had been so recently exposed. He carefully recorded the list of towns in France, Luxembourg, and Germany through which they marched to their assigned sector.

By June of 1919 he was back in the US and finally discharged at Camp Travis in San Antonio. He resumed his pastoral life and duties at the Allen Memorial Presbyterian Church. During his time overseas he had corresponded with his future wife, Myrtle Arthur, a member of his congregation, but it would be almost three years before they would be married.

McLaurin was not a lonely veteran. Plenty of young men from Edna and the surrounding county were returning home, some no doubt turning up in his congregation. For a year, McLaurin resumed his life and pastoral service as it had been before he went off to war. Then came a call came from the Presbyterian church in Sweetwater, Texas. The town was located in a drier climate and was within a three hours' drive of the Texas's tuberculosis sanitarium at Carlsbad. It is possible that McLaurin received outpatient treatment there for his weakened lungs. In any case, he made the move to Sweetwater in 1920.

He was still a bachelor, but that soon changed. On March 2, 1922, he married his long-time sweetheart, Myrtle Alice Arthur. The marriage took place in Dallas and was conducted by McLaurin's friend from Seminary days, Samuel Levinson Joekel, now pastor of a Presbyterian church in nearby Waxahachie. Undoubtedly Myrtle's brother, John Arthur, was in attendance, and thus there was a reunion of sorts; McLaurin had mentioned John's name in his diary as the two crossed paths in France.

Marriage, perhaps, provided the incentive for yet another move, this time to the Presbyterian church in Ballinger, sixty miles or so from Sweetwater. He and Myrtle would remain there for thirteen years, through most of the Depression years, and it would be here that their only child, a son, was born. Lauchlin Arthur McLaurin was born June 27, 1933. His name tells us that the Scottish heritage remained strong among the McLaurins.

In 1932, McLaurin was invited to deliver the baccalaureate address at Daniel Baker College, a small Presbyterian liberal arts college in Brownwood. The degree of Doctor of Divinity was conferred on him during graduation ceremonies the same weekend. Years later, he quipped, "I received a doctorate in exchange for preaching a sermon." In 1936, McLaurin accepted a call to become the Superintendent of Home Missions for Brazos Presbytery, and the McLaurins moved to Houston.

McLaurin, who had remained a dedicated scholar throughout his pastoral ministry, was not especially suited for an administrative position, and his life was soon to take another turn.

In 1938 the call came to join the faculty of his alma mater, The Austin Presbyterian Theological Seminary, and McLaurin was more than prepared both psychologically and intellectually to accept the position.

Academically, his first love was biblical languages, particularly Greek, but for his first six years he was primarily Professor of Systematic Theology. In 1944, James I. McCord was called to assume the responsibilities in all categories of theology and philosophy, which then allowed McLaurin to devote his time to teaching biblical languages and, for a time, church polity (government).

McLaurin was remembered by students as a careful scholar and single-minded in his dedication to teaching. But he was also remembered as an especially gentle friend of students, sometimes too quick to believe a hard-luck story from a student who was about to flunk a course. In any case, every student knew that whatever his own story might be, he would get a hearing from "Dr. Mac." Among his faculty colleagues, he was remembered as supportive, cooperative, and as one who would now be called "a team player," except when he felt he was being pushed too far. Then, he would show the mettle he had demonstrated as a right guard in football many years before.

In 1940 he began his studies for a doctorate in Greek at the University of Texas while carrying his full load of teaching at the seminary. He had little time to immerse himself in his work as a doctoral student, so his program was stretched across twelve years. But, in 1952, he was the first faculty member in the history of the seminary to be awarded a PhD, and only the second recipient of such a rarefied degree in Greek in the history of the University of Texas. He was sixty-four years of age.

Sixty-four years old, yes, but too valuable to be allowed to take retirement at age sixty-five, so he continued to teach until 1958 when he reached seventy.

Retirement and The Final Years

Eugene and Myrtle McLaurin retired to the East Texas town of Waskom where two of his sisters and their husbands resided. He preached in area churches frequently and pursued his one hobby, woodworking. An early task in their large, rambling Federal-style home, one of the oldest houses in Waskom, was to build and replace kitchen cabinets.

The health of both McLaurins declined over time. His poor hearing, an inherited family health issue, diminished further and he eventually wore a hearing aid in each ear. By 1971, both McLaurins needed assisted-living support, so they entered Presbyterian Village in Dallas, where Myrtle died in 1973. Eugene remained there, frequently receiving friends and former students and acting as unpaid chaplain in the nursing wing of the Village. In time, McLaurin left Dallas for Houston to be nearer Lock and his family.

Eugene William McLaurin died on January 23, 1978, five months after his 89th birthday. His body was brought back for burial to Elysian Fields, the little East Texas village where his people had lived for almost seventy years. On Wednesday, January 25, a sizeable congregation filled the old church, the Golden Rule Presbyterian Church, for the mid-morning service. The Rev. Dr. M. L. Baker conducted the service, his selection highly appropriate not only because of friendship stretching back across many decades, but because Baker was also a veteran of World War I. The day was quite cloudy and lighting in the sanctuary was inadequate for anyone attempting to read a Bible passage or even a hymn. Dr. Baker, not long for this world himself, did the best he could, reading passages selected from the King James Version slowly and hesitantly, a pace which somehow gave a certain added dignity to the occasion.

The service ended and the congregation moved from the sanctuary to their cars and in procession drove the 200 yards or so to the New Town cemetery. Snow had begun to fall. The congregation re-gathered quietly and respectfully around the gravesite, Baker then intoning the words of committal. All around were graves of McLaurin's family, and standing in respectful silence were second and third and fourth generations of his family mingled with life-long friends.

These final moments of the service consisted of verses which McLaurin himself had undoubtedly used across the years as an officiating minister; and then a prayer, followed by a familiar benediction. When the congregation lifted their heads, they saw that snow had begun to fall in huge flakes.

A Remembrance: Pastor, Soldier,
Scholar, and Gentleman

McLaurin once taught a seminary class in homiletics (preaching) in the mid-1950s. It was not his academic field; he was simply substituting for the usual professor. Modest man that he was, he suggested sermon ideas but chose not to offer sermon outlines—except one: "The Crossed Hands of God," based on a story from Genesis 48. Joseph, a governor over all of Egypt, brings his two sons to be blessed by their grandfather, Jacob. Jacob places his hands on the heads of Ephraim, the younger, and on Manasseh, the older. But his hands are crossed, his right hand conferring the blessing on Ephraim, the younger. Joseph attempts to move his father's hands, thinking that in his blindness, he has made a mistake. But Jacob replies, "I know it, my son, I know it." The story dovetailed well into the notion of a God whose "ways are past finding out."

Many years later it is impossible to say just why that story meant something special to Eugene McLaurin. Perhaps it had to do with the paradox of a country boy becoming one of the great scholars of New Testament Greek in his generation. Perhaps he was remembering the contradictions of a war so destructive to both sides that the world became numb to its awesome scale, a war where the gentle McLaurin found himself lifting a body for burial in which the blood flooding across the soldier's chest was still warm, and then, a short time later, burying a German soldier after carefully writing down everything he could find on the body to identify the young man. This final regard he made to this German, this member of the nation that had brought Europe and America the Reformation, superb art, literature, and science—and a war more horrible than the world had ever known.

Eugene McLaurin, who sixty years before had learned some deeply painful things about the ambiguities of life, had arrived home—home from the fields of endeavor his church had offered, home from fields of battle, home from the cotton fields—now at rest among his people.

We had celebrated, on that January day in 1978, the life of Dr. Eugene William McLaurin, distinguished scholar and professor of biblical languages, who had also been, many years before, a beloved pastor.

But we were also celebrating the life and military service of Private Eugene William McLaurin. That fact was remembered by few; McLaurin rarely, almost never, referred to his days as a soldier.

At the close of the war and for some months afterward, McLaurin's supervisor, who was also senior chaplain in the 90th Infantry Division, wrote letters to superiors—including two to Congress, asking for a retroactive bestowing of a commission appropriate to the service McLaurin had rendered. But the war was over. Congress and the nation were looking forward, not backward. McLaurin never received a commission. There is evidence that McLaurin himself harbored no regrets. As he once wrote, it had been a privilege to serve under any rank.

Now, a century later, a certain pervasive dignity accrues to McLaurin's humble rank. It includes the traditional, grand military spirit of words like courage and bravery, gallantry and faithfulness to duty. It also embraces the qualities we who knew him remember—a certain abiding humility, an empathy for the worthy student struggling with his courses, a relaxed common sense about what is really important in living a Christian life. In the end, a simpler, more comprehensive word comes to mind in remembering Eugene McLaurin: he was a man of immense grace.

The Diary of Chaplain
Eugene William McLaurin

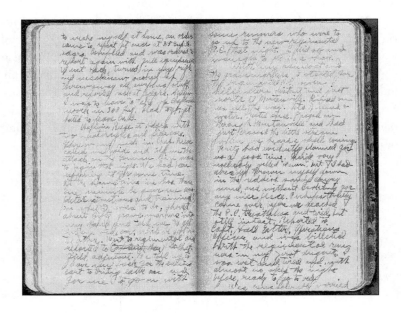

September 9–November 11, 1918

Villers En Haye Sector, St. Mihiel Offensive, Sept. 12–16
Puvenelle Sector, Meuse-Argonne Offensive, Sept. 26-Oct. 1

September 9

Went over to Villers-en-Haye to see Chaplain Reese about applying for a Chaplaincy. Difficult to see him. He advised sending in application and agreed to write Chaplain General, A.E.F., as to necessary steps to take.

Sept. 10

As I had done nothing long enough, I asked to be put on a truck. Relieved Clark on Quarrel's [Quarles's] truck. A wet, rainy day. Hauled two loads of hay from Bellville to Dieulouard.

Sept. 11

Slept in truck. Cold and wet. Quarrels [Quarles] noisy in his sleep. Clark went back on in the afternoon. I went to my billet. The company had moved during the day from Gezancourt to Dieulouard. In room and straw to lie on. There was a church here in which were two air bombs that failed to explode. Had been dropped on the church by the Huns. Had an order, just as I unrolled my blankets and was proceeding to make myself at home, to report at once to the 315th Supply Train Headquarters. Did so, and was ordered to report again with full equipment. Went back, turned in my rifle and mackinaw, packed up, threw away all surplus stuff, and reported back to Headquarters, knowing I was to leave to take up Chaplain work in 360th Infantry. Glad to go, yet hated to leave Co."B."

Chaplain Reese was at Headquarters with two motorcycles and side cars. Threw my pack in.

Chaplain Reese called me inside and told me the attack on the German lines was to begin that night. We had been expecting it for some time. At the same time, in less than one minute, he gave me complete (?) instructions and training (?) in what I was to do, shoved about fifty grave markers into my hand, and told me to get into one side car while he got into the other. Went to Regimental Headquarters and reported to Lt. Chatfield, Adjutant. He told me to leave my pack for the ration cart to bring later on, and for me to go on with some runners who were to go up to the new Regimental P.C. [Post Command] that night. I did so, and managed to get in a shave while we were waiting.

With my rain coat and the grave markers, I started for the Regimental P.C. Seven kilometers distance, and just north of Montauville. Rained on us all the way—lots of mud and water; rested once. Passed on through Montauville, and had just crossed the little stream when we heard a shell coming. Fritz had evidently planned a warm reception for us. Our guide very casually yelled, "down," but I had already thrown myself down in the reddish, sandy mud, without looking for any nice place. Perhaps twenty came over before we reached the P.C. We were breathless, tired, but still all together. Reported to Captain Hall Etter, Operations Officer, and was billeted with the Regimental Runners in my first dug-out. I was wet and tired, and with almost no sleep the night before—ready to get to bed.

Was considerably worried as to what I was to do the next day and succeeding days. No instructions, no special order. Puzzled as to whether I should go over the top next morning. Capt. Etter said wait; so I turned in.

Sept. 12

The real thing has at last come to the Americans. The first operation on a large scale. I was awakened several times for calls for runners to guide troops into positions at the front. One medical detachment became lost, finally pushed on. Later an Infantry Lieutenant with a platoon of men, came in, lost; he dreaded not to be in his position when the barrage opened. He, too, finally went out. At last zero hour came and the barrage began. A battery of 75's, a hundred yards away, began blazing forth at regular intervals. Naval guns about a mile off shook the hill with every shot. The loud reports were almost deafening. The more distant guns sounded like the subdued rumble of thunder.

The boys went over at dawn. Reports of satisfactory progress came in early—prisoners, also. A wounded man came by—a machine gun got him in the shoulder. He wore a rain coat. The Colonel slapped him on the other shoulder as he went to the dressing station.

Uncertain as to what I should do. Reported twice, but told to wait around. So the day finally wore to a close. Apparently our casualties were extremely light; but we reached our objective.

Sept. 13

Lay around until dinner; still nothing to do. Went to dinner; heard that help was needed at an aid station; resolved to go back to ask for permission to help with the wounded. I reported to Capt. Etter and he ordered me to report to the C.O., 1st Bn., 360th Inf. Went with a runner. Passed our old front line positions, through "no-man's land," then through a maze of trench, and at last to 1st Bn P.C., in an old German dug-out. I reported to Major Morris, and was told to report to Cpl. Hirsch, who had charge of the runners—which I did. Supper came later. The scouts brought in many German souvenirs from Vilcey, taken today. Slept in a trench, as Fritz was occasionally shelling. The ground was a mess of shell holes; trenches and barb wire everywhere. Trees all scarred and dead. Everything looks desolate.

Sept. 14

Filled out eight grave location reports. Three men were buried in the woods, and five in German third line trenches. I felt strange in such surroundings. Occasional shelling. Advance showed up. The 1st Bn. in reserve, at 4 o'clock, just as chow came, orders arrive for Bn. to move east in support, behind Norroy, with 3rd Bn., in front. Counter-attack feared. Had pretty good bed, and decided to turn in early, as the march was tiring and we had no food.

Sept. 15

This has been a full day. An unusually fair day, with bright sunshine all day long. Our day's work began at 11 o'clock Saturday night. We were awakened and told to roll packs and fall in immediately. Did so –and waited an hour. So sleepy we could hardly hold our eyes open. Finally started. Stopped for orders at regimental Hq. Once more headed toward the front. Soon came to the end of our road. We had to put on gas masks to go through a mustard gas area, and then wandered around in no-man's land and old German trenches, lost. Finally found a telephone wire and followed it. Reached 3rd Bn. P.C. just at dawn. Then we knew we were to go over. The companies were ordered to prepare, as Major Morris said, for a little open warfare. Bayonets fixed, packs discarded, and we formed for attack. About 7:30 they advanced, and by 8 o'clock has passed over the crest of the hill. I could hardly realize what was taking place. I had the worst experience and feeling of my life. Nothing was said to me at all by any one of the command. I was unattached, with no duty to make me forget myself. Saw Lt. Finkleburg, who had been killed the day before. Saw three other dead men. Saw wounded in three different aid stations, and also by the road-side, waiting for the ambulances. Unnerved and mortally afraid. Fear is doubtless the worst of all sensations. Finally I offered to help the litter bearers. Dr. Newman readily accepted my offer, and I started for the front. Then my fear left me. All that had kept me from seeking a dug-out in the Hindenburg Stellung was a little self-respect.

I saw John Arthur [the writer's future brother-in-law] and Milton Crawford. Helped John carry ammunition across the valley, saw he was tired from the long hike.

I had no other stretcher bearer with me, so I decided to bring in some of the slightly wounded. Many men were already coming in; some severely; others slightly wounded by shrapnel, or gassed. All of them were brave and cheerful. I saw one man from the 359th with two machine gun bullets in his arm. He was smoking a cigarette, and his steadiness brought forth praise even from the doctor.

I went down into the Valley and on through Villers-sous-Preny. I carried John's ammunition almost to the camouflaged road, and then went to the place right down in the valley where some wounded were reported to be. Then about this time the shells began to fall. Before, they had come only intermittently. But now about 11 o'clock, a.m., as the 2nd Bn. came across, they came like hail. As I was up on the hillside, some distance, I had a view of the whole Bn. as it came down the hillside. Although the Germans threw a box barrage around them, they came on, never faltering, never turning back, or even looking toward the rear. By this time, I was in a shell hole, as the shrapnel had begun falling too close. Contrary to my previous ideas, only a very few men were being hit. The shelling increased in violence as the advance came to the foot of the slope. The noise was terrific. The same thing occurred as the 3rd Bn. came across. A machine gun company from the 345th M.G. Bn. passed along just under the sky line, high up on the right hand slope. It seemed as though their activities had for the time being escaped the eyes of the Germans. Suddenly the guns opened up on them and broadside after broadside met them. The 77's, 88's, 155's and some that must have been 10 inches, joined in the deadly chorus. It was terrible. There was the same sublime example of courage; men were simply the superiors of pure physical force and might. Never in all my life was I so proud to be an American. My first intimate knowledge of the German as a fighter shows him to be unfair. He always wants an advantage, and he won't fight when his opponent has anything like an equal chance. For the first time I hated them; our men were helpless; their rifles were useless at such long range. Our artillery did not help. It was moving up and had not established liaison with the infantry. But the German artillery gave us all they had. It rained shrapnel. Even with all these disadvantages, our men conquered. It was a splendid proof of the powerlessness of the most powerful material and physical forces to overcome spiritual qualities of courage, devotion to ideals and willingness for unselfish sacrifice. A man's soul is stronger than all physical forces. This I know now for a truth.

During this time I worked my way to the old farm house on the road from Villers-sous-Preny to Vandiers. Here I found two men gassed. Gas was plentiful in this valley. As the 2nd Bn. came down several gas shells were thrown over. I saw men try to put on their gas masks, but frantically pull them off, because they were out of breath. Some of them had undoubtedly ruined their gas masks when they fell down during the shelling; for this area—right in the valley—was covered with a shallow depth of water. I had to carry these two men across the little creek which came up to my waist, and was extremely cold. About this time there was increased shelling, as we approached the road; compelled us to get into a shell hole. We tried to make ourselves as small as possible, in order to not be hit by any fragments. The enemy had direct observation on us from across the river. Every time we tried to start, more shells would come. We began to think it was all up with us. All of us did some of the most earnest praying that we had ever done. While we were here, I heard a Lieutenant out of the 2nd Bn., which had stopped on account of the heavy shell fire, yell "forward march," and leaped up on the road, crossed over, and went on over with his men. At once they were the targets for the rain of shells, but I saw no one fall. After two hours, we decided to try to go on; we finally succeeded in getting away but concealing ourselves as much as possible. The shelling had decreased, as our objective had been won and held, and men were no longer visible to such a great extent. We walked slowly on account of the gases. Finally we had to get a litter for the M.G. Sergeant. He was badly gassed, and I doubt if he can recover.

My last trip was made down the valley, after supper, just at sun down. We thought we had all the wounded, but wanted to make sure. I found a poor fellow suffering from shell-shock. He thought I was going to kill him, and said he was the unluckiest human alive. He was almost hysterical. I told him to go up the road while I searched the neck of the woods in the Valley and across the creek for wounded. I found none. Earlier in the day I had passed by a man named "Ruder," who had been wounded in the head by a piece of shrapnel. He was unconscious at the time, and I knew that he had only a short time to live. He was dead, and had been moved a few paces by his comrades, who planned to bury him. While over there, I heard a shot and then a scream. At first I thought it was a sniper in the old farm house. I had tried to examine this house, but one room was fastened, and I could not break it open. Extremely careful, I crossed the creek and started toward the man who was crying for help. At last I saw him coming towards me on all fours. When nearer, I recognized him as the shell-shocked man. He was incoherent, almost, but I managed to find out that he had picked up the wrong rifle, and not noticing the hammer, accidentally shot himself through the left foot, in trying to wipe the bayonet on his foot. I cut off his shoe. About this time a stretcher was brought, he was given first aid, and we carried him in. So ended the day's work.

The valley was as peaceful as could be now, with a beautiful moon-lit night. The change from the terrific noise and strife of the day to the silence and peacefulness of the night was hardly believable. I found me a German dug-out, with the opening facing the Germans, and unrolled my pack, and turned in.

Sept. 16

I slept until after eight o'clock. When I waked up, the sun was shining as brightly as anyone could wish for. I was much surprised to learn that during the night the Boches had laid over a heavy barrage of shrapnel and gas. I saw some of the effects in the shattered trees along the road and in the big shell holes, although I was sleeping in a hole that was facing in the direction, it did not even wake me. I was dead to the world.

Shaved, rolled my pack, left a note on it that I was coming after it later, and got breakfast.

Then I went across the valley, and finally found the 1st Bn. P.C., which was a concrete pill box. I reported to Maj. Morris, who desired to know why I did not stay with his staff, and then to Lt. Hartell, Bn.

Adj., who commended me for doing as I did. I buried two men just at dark. One was killed by a German canteen. He had evidently picked up somewhere a German canteen that was loaded; he attempted to open it and there was an explosion. One side of the canteen was blown into pieces; the other side remained intact. Unluckily for him, he was on the side blown out, and a fragment of metal killed him. His name was Jimmy Givas. The other was Cpl. R.R. King, 315 F.S. Bn. I hated to go after my pack, but had it to do. I found everything scattered. Only my overseas cap was missing, however. I slept in trench with runner.

Sept. 17

Buried Clarence H. Braschel, and parts of an unidentified body. Only one leg and the head could be found. The head had been blown up into a tree, 40 feet away. I moved to a pill-box to sleep.

Late in the afternoon, just at supper time, the Germans shelled Villers-sur-Preny heavily. Their observers had evidently seen chow details entering the town where the kitchens were located. At first the shelling was light, but increased quickly. I was in Company "D's" kitchen at the time, trying to get something to eat. A mess cup and a spoon were all the dishes I had. I carried them with me all the time. I had the mess cup filled with "slum" when the shelling began. The kitchen was in an old barn, and on the side toward the Germans there was a thick wall. At once we all scattered and tried to find a safer place. We ran into a cellar. We had been there only a few minutes when gas shells began coming over and we had to put on our gas masks. The air was full of dust and H.E. [high explosions] gas, together with poisonous gas. All the food had been ruined, as gas had done its work. The chow details had to take corn willy, tomatoes and hard tack to the boys up at the front. I kept on my gas mask for half an hour and as the shelling had almost subsided I decided to go back to my pill-box. Several shells fell as I left town, and I ran into a strong concentration of mustard gas. I had to put on my gas mask, and I was entirely out of breath when I reached the pill-box. This is one time I did without supper.

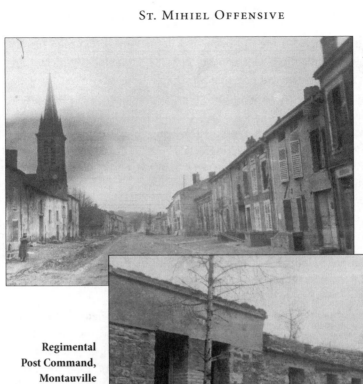

Main street of
Montauville

Regimental
Post Command,
Montauville

German machine gun
belts and barbwire on
road around hill from
Norroy to Vandieres
and Villers-sous-Preny

Trenches in stone quarries south of Villers-sous-Preny

Wire entanglements
in the Quarries

Church at Norroy

Road through
no-man's land in
Bois-le-Pretre

German
ammunition

Battalion Aid Station
in "Death Gulch"

Removing the dead from the
trenches; photograph courtesy
of the Library of Congress

Grave of Supply Sgt. John J. Roggemon

Sept. 18

Two men of Co. "C", Long and Filligen, [were] killed by terrific shell fire [during the night] on Hill 327. Sgt. Karbowski [was] severely wounded at the same time and taken to the first-aid station. He died as the operation was finished. We buried Long and Filligen on the steep reverse slope of Hill 327. It was extremely difficult to dig the graves on account of the steepness of the Hill at this place, but we had to stay under cover in order to not imperil any more lives. The digging was several times interrupted by the firing of troublesome whiz-bangs. They were timed to burst in the air, just over the trenches. Several times shrapnel came down where we were. Just as we finished covering the graves, and I had read part of a verse from Corinthians, two more came in quick succession and burst directly overhead. All the details left without further ceremony, and so did I. It is senseless to expose one's self uselessly.

Later in the day a corporal [Williams] from Hq. Co. and I started back across the valley to fill out a grave location blank for Sgt. Hall E. Irwin, of Hq. Co., who was killed Sept. 14th, and was buried by a Y.M.C.A. man. We had gone only a short distance and were talking about various things when our conversation was suddenly interrupted. An aeroplane had been coasting around above us, and although we had been frequently warned, we were not in the habit of taking cover, I paid no attention to it. I did not think it was a danger. Suddenly he opened up on us with a machine gun. By cutting off his engine and diving, he had approached within a few hundred feet of us. We jumped over at once to a stone wall and tried to protect ourselves. The bullets were striking the road and also the limbs of trees over us. After this no aeroplane gets a shot at me if I see it first. We went to Sgt. Irwin's grave, and I filled in the location blank, and also the grave location blanks for some other men who had been killed earlier in the drive.

Sept. 19

With detail of prisoners from Hq. Co., we went down to Vandieres today and buried two Poles from the 82nd Division (in the outskirts of Vandieres). The bodies were in an advanced stage of decomposition. Both men had evidently been killed in the drive Sunday morning. They had taken cover in a sunken road, and two shells landed near them, one in the soft dirt of a vineyard, and the other on a rocky surface. It was the latter shell that killed them. Two of the boys went into the town for boards to make grave crosses. While in town they saw many reminders of the fight, among them, dead horses, rabbits, a cat, and some dead Germans. We also buried Sgt. Karbowski by the road through Death Valley. This road early received this name from the men because it was constantly shelled day and night. It was dangerous to pass up and down this road at any time. Many horses had been killed, though several were wounded.

Sept. 20

I loafed this morning. I discovered two concealed dug-outs, and the entrance to one of them was a machine gun. I could not explore them on account of water in the passages and rooms. I believed they were joined together by a tunnel. There were several German packs here. I opened them, but found nothing especially interesting. After dark we buried Cpl. Spath and Fate Holland of "C" Co., who had been killed Sunday morning when a shell fell in the midst of a combat group. We picked up on the ground around them seven rifles. Evidently only one man of the squad was able to continue the advance after the shell struck. We had to bury them at night on account of the bodies being in direct observation of the enemy's balloons. Cpl. Spath was the Champion grenade thrower of the 360th Regiment. German planes with signal lights were patrolling, and we were constantly in fear that they would open their tail-end-gates and unload on us. Sgt. Bishop sent a man to this combat group to take a burning and exploding cartridge belt off a man whose arms were useless. As to what happened to this man, nothing is known. In speaking of him, Sgt. Bishop said, "He was a church member, and sure was a good boy—not rough, like the rest of us guys."

Sept. 21

At last relief has been made. 3rd Bn. 360(th) has gone in, and we have come back to near Montauville. I never was so tired in all my life. Slept with Isaacs, a Co. "D" runner, and Watts, a "B" Co. Runner. The three of us slept together, and as they were both big men and I was small—and on the outer edge, there was very little cover for me, and I slept cold that night. We got up at noon. Everybody was tired and sore and worn out.

Sept. 22

At dusk we moved back to Jezainville. Here I found a fairly good place for a good bed. No services today. All of us were too tired to exert ourselves, except under compulsion. The exposure, exertion and gas leaves us weak and with no endurance.

Sept. 23

I bought a can of cherries today in a typical French shop and paid the typical French price of eight francs. High, but anything sweet, no matter what it costs. I have about fifteen francs yet. It is fine to sleep inside on a bed.

It was up on the St. Mihiel salient that the Germans played a daring trick on us. It was not far from our positions to the Moselle River. Every night a launch would come up the river and simply shell us to death. It could maneuver and reach almost all our positions. Finally it was discovered by a patrol out in the valley. The solution was found to [?] the mysterious gun which seemed so near and could not be located. Later Sgt. Bishop of Co. ? volunteered with several others to capture it one night if an officer would go along. Lt. Wright volunteered. When night came, the sergeant and his men were ready but no officer appeared.

Another mystery was also solved about this same time. Some 77's were firing on us from nearby and it was apparently impossible to locate them. One night a patrol advanced quite a distance toward the enemy positions. With them was an artillery officer with glasses. They advanced to such a position that they could see these gun positions. That night they could see flash after flash of the guns. The artillery officer secured the coordinates. The next day our artillery destroyed a barn and with it a battery of enemy artillery.

Sept. 24

Chaplain Lewis came down. He advises me to lose no time in getting in my application for a commission. I don't know whether to push it or not. I believe a man can do about as good work without a regular commission. Grapes are getting ripe in the vineyards, and we buy lots of them. That is about all we can buy. Sometimes the Y.M.C.A. has something, but not very much for each one.

Sept. 25

Fritz gave us a lively shelling last night. It was the first serenade that we have experienced since coming off the front. Two 77 shells struck the church just across the street, but did little damage. One large shell hit the corner of Lt. Hartell's room. Several of the boys went down to the dug-out. I thought once I would go; but I felt that the shells would miss me, so instead I turned over and went to sleep. But the shells woke me up regularly every fifteen minutes.

Sept. 26

I went to Montauville and was examined for a commission, "paper examination." I had recommendations from Maj. Morris, from Col. Price, and from Chaplain Reese. So everything is ready.

Sept. 27

I filed my application this afternoon. Have written lots of letters this week. It was time. For we have been so busy lately that no one has had a chance to write letters.

Sept. 28

Nothing much to do today. We're glad to find out that we don't have to go back until tomorrow night. All of us are happy at another day back here. Not one wants to go back to the front. One trip is enough. No man in his senses wants to go a second time.

Sept. 29

We had our services today in a back hall. About 40 or 50 men were present. Mr. McDowell, of Boston, did the talking. We moved up to the front again, at least, to support position. There were several stragglers along the way. I brought the gun of one all the way from Jezainville. He never offered to take it back, and is sleeping tonight in a dug-out. Sorry worthless fellow. We have a good dug-out and I have a German bed. This place must have been used for an aid station.

Sept. 30

I spent the morning in acquainting myself with our new position. To the
left is Villers. To the right is Norrey. To the front is an intricate labyrinth
of trenches which the Germans dug. Our dug-out is as near bomb-proof
as any I have ever seen. It was used by the Germans for a hospital. It has
three exits; so even if a shell closes one, we can get out at one of the others. Eight letters came today, the first mail, except two or three letters at
Jezainville, that I have had since leaving the supply train.

October 1

A beautiful day, bright and sun-shiny; Sgt. Gunstreet, of the Scouts, said
there was a fine frost; I got up too late to see it.

As many of the men had asked me when the Y. M. C. A. was going
to bring something to them I decided to make a trip to Montauville and
managed to bring up enough to give everyone a taste of chocolate and
cigarettes. Also brought some newspapers as news is exceedingly scarce
in the front lines. As a result of Bulgaria's unconditional surrender, important developments in the Central Powers may be expected soon, in
the opinion of everyone.

Oct. 2

I was sore all over from packing that Y. M. C. A. stuff. But I had to go back
today to complete arrangements for sending Y. M. C. A. supplies to the
companies by the ration trucks.

I saw Devenfont White yesterday and again today. I took dinner with
him. As we were coming back from dinner, we were greatly surprised to
meet Gerald Meeks. He had come down from Thiaucourt, which place
this division, the 5th, held. He said he had not been able to wash his face
for several days. Not even shaving water.

Oct. 3

I spent most of the day exploring Norroy. This town had been full of machine gun nests before the drive, but our artillery was ordered to throw a
heavy fire into the town, and soon silenced the machine guns. The town

gave plenty of evidence of the effects of our artillery fire. Many of the houses were blown all to pieces, and more of them had holes in the walls or roofs. It was apparently a resting place for Bosch officers, as children's and women's clothes were seen in the greatest abundance. Most of these were of excellent material. There was also a large library of costly bound books. Most of the books were technical, and did not contain so very much fiction; apparently the whole library was for the sick, there being a surgical room adjoining in which were found some surgical instruments.

The church was pretty badly torn up. All the windows were shattered. Two shells had come in near the Altar; but the Altar itself had escaped. Already the French had been in the town and had set up a figure of Joan of Arc in battle armor, draped with the French flag, in the church. These monuments or statues of the heroine are to be seen in every church.

As I was standing in the shattered doorway, a figure came out lower down the street, which was as unusual, and unexpected then as a South-Sea Islander in native costume in the crowded streets of New York. Inside "it" was an American soldier; outside it seemed to be a society swell, with high stove pipe hat, claw-hammer coat and black trousers, with his hat sat on the side of his head—and twirling a cane—he came promenading down the street. It was ridiculous. Everything else was grey. The soldier dude made a lively contrast.

I was afraid of shelling while I was in the town, as there were many men moving about on the streets. Several kitchens, also of the 2nd Bn., were in the place, in easy observation of the enemy. However, no shells came over.

Oct. 4

Chaplain Lewis came up today, to get me to go down and swear to my application before an officer to administer an oath. So at least it is off—my application.

Oct. 5

A terrible day. All day long the Germans shelled our positions, as they had exact information of this sector; they send them over accurately whenever and wherever they want to. Two big guns from the fortifications around Metz have been firing on us all day and have fired on us all day at

15 minutes intervals. No report could be heard. With them always came the 88's from across the river. Some engineers, filling up shell holes in the road behind the P.C., evidently startled the Huns. The first shell struck at the bridge across the trench. Joiner, a runner, and I were just coming back from the kitchen, where we had been to get water. They came rather too close for comfort; so we went into the dug-out and stayed in most all the rest of the day. Several times shells hit near the P.C., and one time the violence of the concussion forced open a heavy door. With each explosion a distinct tremor could be felt in the earth. No one was wounded, however, until about dusk; then a big H.E. landed on "B" Company's P.C. and caved in one room. In this room at the time were three or four men. Drohan and Conley were killed instantly, and the other escaped injury, but was seriously shell-shocked. Little, a Bn. runner, who was standing in the door from the other room, was blown by the force of the explosion into the other room. He also suffered shell-shock. I went down as soon as it was reported at the P.C. Capt. Hogg was distinctly nervous. Also was everybody else. Already one squad was trying to recover the bodies in hope that life might still be found. Drohan's body was soon recovered from the wreckage. But it was impossible to get Conley's body. Poor fellow, about four feet of rock and debris fell on him.

With another squad I started digging the graves, where Sgt. Irwin's body was buried. When I came back to the P.C. the litter bearers came up with Drohan's body. He was terribly mangled, the shrapnel having gone into his chest, and warm blood was soaking all over his clothes. I felt horrified when I felt the warm liquid; but I searched every pocket for personal effects, just for the sake of his folks back home. The more I see of this hellish business the more deeply I hate war.

As we were filling in the graves, the boys got to talking about what a change the last few weeks had made in their lives. Three said it had made real Christians of them. It gave me a queer feeling out there in the darkness and danger, to hear men talking so frankly. I wonder how many of these good resolutions will be remembered in real life.

Lt. Hartell went up several notches in my estimation tonight. It was just after the runner from regimental Headquarters came, with the usual bunch of orders. The Sgt. Major called for runners from every company. Shells were still falling outside, and no one was anxious to leave the dugout, but Lt. Hartell happened to hear him and acted at once. He asked if there was anything important, and proceeded to see for himself. When he had looked through the papers, he said for them to wait until morning. Everyone breathed a sigh of relief.

Sgt. Gunstream, who deserted the scouts and came to our dugout, had to go to the O. P. tonight. He seems anxious for peace on any terms.

Oct. 6

Sunday, and naturally our moving day. Tonight, just after dark, we took up front line position, relieving the 2nd Battalion. We passed through "Death Valley" just in time to miss a severe shelling from Fritz. Joiner was helping to set the pace, and we made it in double-quick time. We had to police-up our pill-box before we could make down our bunks. Policing, it seems, is always with us.

Buried Connely [Conley] just at daybreak. We did not want Fritz to catch us at work, as he could make it extremely unpleasant. Connely was a Catholic, and his widowed mother's only son. He did not have to come, either; but he insisted on being sent, although he seemed to know something of the coming death. He said all the time that he would never go back.

Oct. 7

I spent most of the day up on the front. I saw the sumptuous dug-out of which I have heard so much in the last two weeks. This dug-out was division headquarters for the Germans in this area. It is a fine example of the labor of our enemies. They must have used their periods of rest in this sector in building dug-outs, trenches, pill-boxes, etc., I wonder why they have not shelled it, as they must know that we are using it. Some day they will get it.

Saw John Arthur. He is getting along all right.

Oct. 8

I went out on a tour of exploration today in Vandieres. It is a sort of no-man's land. Although it is within our area, we have only an advanced patrol in the far end of the town. This is another town that the Germans left in a hurry. Everything was scattered pell-mell, and some of the rabbits had been left to die in their cages. In a few houses the meal was served and ready to be eaten. In one or two places in the street the odor from dead animals was unendurable.

I brought back several souvenirs; one was a glass of jam, which was greatly appreciated. It is queer that we get so hungry for sweets up on the front. In a room where there were religious tracts in profusion, I found a soft, pure white wool blanket. From the appearance of the place, I guess its owner must have corresponded closely to one of our Y.M.C.A. men. At any rate, this blanket will do service in the near future for a dough-boy in an American Army. I hope I can manage to get home with it, as it would be a rare souvenir. In an officer's quarters I found a fine, heavy cane, which I brought back with me. I have an idea that it will prove extremely helpful to me on future hikes, as the roads are always muddy, and the hills are hard to climb with a pack. We are to be relieved tomorrow night by the 7th Division. Well, it's time!

Oct. 9

As this was our last day on this front, I paid a farewell visit to Hill 327. I took a last look at Preny, Chateau-de-Preny, and Pagny-sur-Moselle. The valley of the Moselle River from Hill 327 North affords a beautiful view. I took a look through some artillery glasses and saw a road along which there was occasionally some traffic. The drivers often desert their wagons under our artillery fire, which is accurate and effective. Far away, on a hill side, is a vineyard. As grapes are ripe now, our friends, the enemy, decided to gather them; but after a few shots from our artillery into this particular vineyard, they changed their minds, and left their grapes, and also some of their dead friends.

Chaplain Lewis called me late this afternoon by telephone to support position P.C. The graves registration man was there. I came over and made my last trip, I hope, through Death Valley. Just as I passed the Spring, which had been badly shot up, Fritz sent over four 77's. They struck about 50 yards behind me. I saw them hit, and fragments whizzed through the air striking the trees around. I had jumped into a shell hole, but decided that I would watch them. I have made many trips through this valley safely, but each time was a test, for it was constantly shelled. Every time I have passed through it during the past two weeks, I have thought of the verse: "Verily I will walk through the Valley of the Shadow of Death; I will fear no evil." I found the graves registration man, and gave him information concerning the location of the graves of all the men that I had buried.

Then Chaplain Lewis, the Chaplain of the 56th Infantry, and I came on to Montauville together. It was one of the muddiest trips that I have ever made, and the new Chaplain was in "Sam Brown Belt," russet shoes, leather leggings, and serge uniform. He fell down and ruined all his fine togs in that awful Bois le Pretre. As he fell, I said "whoa!" He was a true sport, and answered back, "Too late now!" I got a bite to eat at Regimental Headquarters, and came on to Jezainville for a bed and a good long night's sleep.

Oct. 10

We have said farewell to this sector. I want to get to some new country and see some new things and new surroundings.

I left Jezainville about 10 o'clock with all my equipment and came to where the Battalion had marched to during the night, about two miles south of Jezainville. I arrived just in time to get a good meal. At exactly 12 o'clock, we started out again, marching back, we hoped to a rest camp. Soon the country showed no evidences of the terrible conflict. There was no longer desolation, the shell-holes, dead and mutilated trees, and the loneliness of the front lines. Everything is quiet, and it seems as though we have suddenly entered another world. Civilians are attending to the work of various kinds, agriculture, etc. The sun came out this afternoon for the first time, it seems to me, in several weeks. We greeted its appearance with expression of hope and cheer, since it seemed to welcome us back to civilization. The roads were heavy today, so the majority of us got tired enough to stay in close. We stopped at Pierre-St. Ettienne, about 5 miles from Toul.

Oct. 11

We finished the march to the rear, and went into billets in barracks in Domgermain. My feet almost gave out on me on the last lap of the journey. My tendons of Achilles have about broken in two. I think it is caused by having so much mud to walk through. The mud is everywhere, even on the paved highways. The battalion headquarters detachment has been called the "walking-stick brigade," as almost every member has a walking stick. No one can imagine how much real help a walking stick is in making these long hikes. I think mine shall be a constant companion from now on.

This town is on a hill-side, almost at the foot of the hill. There are several high hills around the town, and we are told that there are forts and big-guns on each one of them. Vineyards cover the hill-sides and the people are at work, gathering the grapes. They come in every evening with baskets and big vats filled with grapes. Then they run the grapes through a crushing machine and put them into a big cask, holding between 200 and 250 gallons. Sometimes the crushing is done by stamping in them or wading around in them with heavy shoes on—nice and clean! But I don't drink the wine.

Oct. 12

This was rest day. Everyone was too tired to do anything but loaf around, and almost too tired to do that. I lay on my bunk most of the day, and so did the others. The nights are getting cold now, and I almost freeze every night. We have to double up at night, and sometimes treble. Nichols, Joiner and I are trying it together at present, and it proves a satisfactory arrangement.

Oct. 13

We had services at the Y.M.C.A. morning and evening. Both services were well attended. An enlisted man of the Ammunition Train spoke tonight. He was a manly appearing fellow, and is just out of college. After the services, Cpl. Bond, of "D" Company, went up and met him, together with myself. He is a Methodist.

Austria's note to Wilson has created quite a fever, and the wildest rumors are current today. Some think that peace is almost here, and that the Central Powers will collapse in only a few days. The hope is fervently expressed that peace, or something else, will come, so that we won't have to go back to another front. I have not heard a man say that he wanted to go back and try those things again.

By a very narrow margin we missed being sent to Verdun last night. An order came out for us to be ready to load on the trucks by 8 o'clock, and the trucks, we were told, were already on the way. We were heartbroken at the prospect of being sent into action again; because we knew that we would not be moving so early if we were not going into an active sector. About 7 o'clock, though, an order came in countermanding the previous one; so we went to sleep contentedly.

Oct. 14

I managed for new clothes today.

Oct. 15

I wrote several letters today; went over to Choloy this afternoon, and saw several old friends in the old battalion. Tomorrow we leave for Verdun.

Oct. 16

We piled into French trucks today and made a leap of about 60 kilometers. It was cold and chilly, but I managed to stay warm. We had some bread along, and someone had managed for a can of butter. So we had plenty to eat on the way. The roads were muddy as usual. At dark we unloaded about a half mile from our destination, some old French barracks in the Bois-de-St. Pierre. But in trying to reach them, also as usual, and a necessary part of the schedule, we got lost. We wandered about two hours, or maybe three. During part of this time the rain was falling hard. We finally reached the barracks, and there was a wild scramble for bunks, or for places to spread blankets; as the roof leaked badly.

For the most of us it was a night of considerable discomfort. The leaking water either fell on us from the room, or it ran under the barracks and was on the ground, on which we were lying. The kitchens got lost— also a necessary part of the schedule—so we had to do without supper. There was a lot of grumbling, which was to be expected, inasmuch as we had had only one hot meal during the day. But most all of us had managed for a little bit extra before we left Domgermain. So we pulled that out and made it do for supper.

Oct. 17

I moved into a better shack today, with Joiner and some of the others. It, at least, has a floor, does not leak, and has an improvised fireplace in the middle of the room. The smoke becomes extremely uncomfortable at times, as we have no pipe or stove. By staying low we can remain in the room and keep comfortable. The kitchens arrived in time to give us supper.

Oct. 18

I went over to Blyercourt, about two miles away, and brought over some papers for the battalion. Everyone, myself included, is extremely anxious to keep up with events during these days. We are still in hopes that in some way or other we won't have to go to the front again. The Y.M.C.A. brought in some supplies today, and although everything was soon sold, it at least partly satisfied our longing for sweets. "Dad" Holman asked me to take charge of it and I did.

Oct. 19

I went over for the papers again tonight. When I came back several men from the 2nd Battalion and also men from the 345th Machine Gun Battalion were waiting for papers. A bosche plane came over last night and planted several bombs on the hill. Lights out, by orders, of course, and I was glad; for I hate the purring of their engines. Nothing seems more terrifying than this droning sound as they pass over me. It reminds me more of some animal of the cat tribe, and is just as dangerous and treacherous.

Oct. 20

I held two services today; in the morning "A" and "B" companies gathered in the barracks with "A" Company, and Sgt. Moreland of "A" Company led in singing. In the afternoon Companies "C" and "D" held services. It certainly had rained today. All day long it has poured down with only short intermissions. I went over after the papers again. This is the last time. I don't know when we will ever get any more news. For we will go up again on the front tomorrow.

Oct. 21

We left the old French barracks today and moved up toward the front. As we marched away in columns of two's, the band played for us. It was inspiring and encouraging, for we knew that we would endure much before they would be with us again, and many of the boys would never see them again. Our line of march led us near Verdun. We could see the fierceness of the struggle which stopped the men of the Crown Prince in 1916. Numberless graves with French markings showed the price France paid. We also saw several recent graves of Americans with helmets of the owners. The incessant traffic and the mud make marching slow and tiresome.

We passed through one town which is closely associated with the famous Verdun battle. This town was Avocourt, of which not a single wall remained standing. One would scarcely notice that even it had at one time been a town, so complete was the destruction.

American engineers were getting stones for the roads, which are being built to carry our continually passing trucks. On the left was Hill 304, we were told. The destruction in this area was the worst I ever saw and defies description. It is the most desolate place imaginable, and it is difficult to see how vegetable or wild animal life can be sustained here. However, the places teem with American soldiers. There is no place in sight that does not show khaki. I thought I saw Gerald Meeks this afternoon, but I am not sure. He was horse-back. I was so busy making my way through the mud that I didn't have time to look around. And at that time a moving kitchen jammed us out of the road into a ditch; so I didn't have time to ascertain for sure whether or not it was he.

Oct. 22

We stayed all day where we camped last night, in the edge of the Argonne. It was somewhat damp this morning, but we had put up our pup-tents. So we slept fairly warm. Just at sun-down, we moved out, going toward the front. It was extremely dark, but we got on the road before the deepest darkness came on. Orders had been given, and were strictly enforced, with regard to stragglers; no man was to be allowed to drop out. Every time the Major saw a man unattached, he inquired as to what organization he belonged to. One such man failed to make any response, and the Major spoke sharply to him, asking him his name and organization again. He proved to be a man from "D" Company, who had lost his voice as a result of measles, and could not speak above a whisper. Lt. Hartell recognized him and put the Major straight. We passed through Montfauson, where the Germans were only a few weeks before. This place had offered a strong resistance, and was captured only after fierce fighting.

We camped for the night at the edge of the Bois-de-Veuge, about a mile north of Montfauson. It was too late to go into the woods, so we had to make down our bunks as best we could. We put our shelter-halves on the ground to keep out the dampness and mud and managed to sleep fairly well.

Oct. 23

We had to get up early, before good daylight. We had made down our bunks in the open, and any wandering Hun air-man could easily pick us up and give our location to the artillery. We are about 10 kilometers from the front.

Oct. 24

Chaplain Lewis came over in the evening, and we went over to Montfaucon. It was at this place that the German Crown Prince nervously watched the progress of the Verdun drive over two years ago. This town is a vantage point, an excellent view is obtained of the surrounding country for miles and miles. It was where the remains of the concrete periscopic tower from the cellar of which the Crown Prince watched the battle. It rained gently most of the night. I threw my shelter-half over my face; but it suffocated me, and I had to leave my face half uncovered.

Oct. 25

It rained all night last night; but we had our shelter-halves up, so we slept fine. Several shells came over last night; but almost all of them were duds. I counted nine duds out of thirteen that came over, during one period of shelling. Over across the valley are some 105's left by the Germans in the last drive. They must have left in a hurry, as the guns were not destroyed. On this hill also were several; but every one of them has been rendered useless.

Oct. 26

The Germans sent over more shells today. One hit right in a bunch of the men who were bringing up some rations. Dirt and shell fragments flew everywhere, but no one was injured. There were some other narrow escapes during the day. I see John A[rthur] every day.

Oct. 27

Chaplain Lewis and I held five services today. We tried to cover the whole regiment, and I think succeeded fairly well. In the main, they were largely attended. Action is imminent, and every one knows and feels it. Shells fell while we were having the services. Several aerial bursts today made us dodge. The Catholic priest came over and held confessions for the Catholic men. There was quite a line-up. I noticed several officers lined up to receive the priest's blessings before going into action.

Oct. 28

The shelling last night was rather severe and prolonged; several of the boys moved into a shallow, broad ditch. I did not move, but slept through most of the shelling. Occasionally a loud one would wake me. Some of those big ones must have come from a long distance. It is remarkable how safe one feels when shells are falling with only the frailest covering for a protection. I had only my pup-tent, but I felt reasonably safe. After each explosion I would turn over and go to sleep again.

Oct. 29

We moved up again soon to relieve the 179th Brigade, which had been in the front-line position quite a bit now. The officers and some of the runners went up today to look over the positions. They report artillery on every hill and in every valley. Evidently a big attack is being planned and our Brigade will be in at the start-off. We can do it, if we have to; but no one is anxious to be in another battle. I saw some Frenchmen today, and they say that with Austria's last note, the war will be over in fifteen days. I haven't much respect for their opinion; but I hope they are right.

Oct. 30

We moved up tonight to the wooded hill northwest of Romagne. Division headquarters is in this town. We are billeted in the edge of the Argonne Forest, and it doesn't look very safe to me tonight. We are told that we may as well expect pretty heavy shelling.

Oct. 31

We had some severe shelling last night, as the Germans are actively searching out our artillery. No one was killed, or even seriously wounded. Six boys in Company "C" had a miraculous escape, though. The six of them lay down with their heads next to a clump of bushes; they hung their rifles up in the trees. Sometime during the night a big shell came over and hit on the other side of the clump of trees. Most of the trees were cut off even at the ground. Several of the rifles were hopelessly ruined, and one was never found.

I went over to Regimental Headquarters early this morning. Chaplain Lewis was burying some men killed by shell fire during the night. This was in the valley just behind our front line positions. I saw one American lieutenant, and a number of soldiers, and quite a number of Germans, who were killed a few days ago in the fighting here. They were still unburied, although they must have been dead at least 10 days, maybe two weeks. Several of the Germans were mere boys, apparently not over 18 years of age.

The big barrage begins tonight at 3:30 a.m. We get up and turn in surplus equipment and make our packs at 2:30. It will be quite a lively Halloween part. The 3rd Battalion goes over the top at 5:30; the 2nd Battalion will go over later in the 2nd wave, and the 1st Battalion will follow in the last wave. Who can tell what will happen by this time tomorrow night? Many a one of our fellows will be killed. It seems horrible to think of men so full of life meeting death in such a short time.

November 1

This has been a long and terrible day. During the night the enemy shelled our area continually. A battery of 75's was located about 200 yards to our left, and the Germans knew their positions. This battery was shelled off and on all during the night. One shell made a direct hit and put one of the guns out of commission. One man was killed and several wounded. But so far as I know, none of our men was wounded during the night. Shrapnel was whizzing around us all night long, and I was expecting that the Battalion would suffer at least light casualties. Some of the shells were big H.E.'s and shook the earth with their explosion.

At 2:30 sharp everyone was awakened and ordered to roll packs. All surplus baggage was to be salvaged. I salvaged a new over-coat, a fine German blanket of soft wool, which I had found in Vandieres, and my little Bible. I am afraid that I will never see them again. But I can't take them with me. After rolling our packs, we made ourselves as comfortable as possible and settled down to wait until the big show would break loose at 3:30. Hirsch, Glenn, and I had a frail shelter with the protection given by a frail door above us. Some of the boys had fox holes, which they had dug, and covered over with brush and earth. They were extremely cold and wet. We nearly froze, as we had only our rain-coats for extra cover. We wondered how we would fare when the barrage started.

At last, all at once, the artillery broke loose along the front in both directions. There were three batteries of 75's near us, and their constant "spank-spank" made talk impossible. The sky in all directions was a steady glow with these flashes, each one lasting only a second, but coming from literally thousands and thousands of cannon mouths. It seemed as though every valley and ravine had its battery and was taking its share of the deadly work. Along with the 75's and 155's could be heard at rare intervals—although even at that, rather often—the deep booming of the heavies of naval guns, as we assumed them to be. It is easy enough to distinguish them.

A heavy artillery bombardment is indescribable, I believe. It is too big, too tremendous; the sound is intense and constant. Conversation is impossible at close quarters. And even then the noise is beyond description. The greatness, the bigness and the terribleness of such a united fire give the individual that feeling of littleness and powerlessness. He is absolutely helpless when opposed by them. Still, men are operating these tremendous forces themselves. And all these great forces wait for man to will them before they operate.

When our barrage began, of course the enemy opened up, also. More shells fell in our immediate vicinity, and the same fragments filled the air after each explosion. Several fragments hit around us, and on our improvised tents. Their force was usually spent, though, by the time they arrived in our immediate neighborhood. One murderous looking piece struck just about a foot from our heads. Another little piece hit me on the head. It is a wonder many of us were not wounded; but we were lucky enough to escape unscathed.

A little before 5:30, zero hour for the attack, we went out in single file, and moved up toward Regimental Headquarters. As we left the woods, several shells, intended for the battery, fell within a few yards of us, and several men were wounded. However, we were soon out of the area being shelled. At one time we had to veer around so as not to pass directly in front of a battery of our own artillery. It was beginning to get day, and a murky haze came over everything.

As we came to the second road leading out of Bantheville toward the West, the 2nd Battalion under Major Etter was just leaving, going over as a second wave. We dived into holes which they had just vacated and found quite a good shelter up under the bank. Enemy shells were falling thick along this road, as the enemy rightly guessed it to be a fine place for the concentration of the reserved troops. Up in the edge of the woods our Battalion lost several men from this artillery fire.

We had not been here long before we saw some light artillery moving up to take up more advanced positions. Someone remarked, "The artillery is going over with the dough-boys." It was certainly true. In perhaps not over an hour after the first wave had gone over the artillery was taking up positions in what had been a short hour or so before no-man's land. Evidently the attack was entirely successful and good progress was being made.

While here we saw the first fruits of our success, and also the quick progress of our troops. Prisoners began passing to the rear. At first in groups of two or more, and later 40 or 50 at a time—they came! Then we learned the news that the initial attack was a complete success. The Freya Stellung, the last organized defenses of the Hun, was broken.

Most of the prisoners had thrown away their helmets as soon as they surrendered. It seemed queer to us that they should do this, even though the artillery fire was heavy around them. Practically all of them seemed glad that it was over, and all were relieved to be assured of safety. Sometimes they would be bringing our wounded in on stretchers. Stretchers were not always on hand, so frequently they improvised serviceable substitutes out of poles and blankets. They brought in several of their own wounded on such stretchers.

Several times the Germans came towards the rear, unattended by guards. They often hid until the assaulting troops had passed over and then surrendered to the first passer-by. One bunch of 22 wanted to surrender to John Boyd of Lavaca [Texas]– now in "I" Company. He was a litter bearer, and unarmed, I believe, and would not allow them to approach near him, but motioned them to the rear, where they obediently went.

Several of our wounded were brought down this road on stretchers, and quite a few of the walking wounded passed along this way. Among the walking wounded was Lt. Buck J. Wynne, until recently of Co. "B", but now assigned to Co. "M". A machine gun bullet got him in the thigh. He was always whistling and cheerful when he was in Co. "B". As he passed, he gave us a warm smile, and the aid man helping him to the first-aid station said that he had tried to whistle. He was weak from shock and exhaustion, but was brave to the very last.

As it seemed likely that we were to stay here for some time, I felt that I ought to be doing something somewhere. Col. Price had given orders that Chaplain Lewis and I were to stay behind with a detail and bury the men killed in action. I felt that there were wounded men upon the battlefield who needed help, and finally I went up to the Regimental P.C. to see what could be done. I hid my pack, and then I found Chaplain Lewis and asked him what orders he had for me. He told me that we were to wait for the detail. Shells were still falling around, and I did not think that any detail would report that day for burying. About that time Capt. Maxwell and Sgt. Kennedy, of Hq. Co., came in from the front, almost without breath. I asked for news, and especially if there were any wounded. Sgt. Kennedy said there were many wounded, both our own and Germans, who were asking for help, or even water. I resolved to go to the front at once, and said as much to Chaplain Lewis. He smiled, and said, "Go to it. I'll stay here, and I think I can do all this work anyway." So I took my departure, going over the hill with nothing besides my raincoat and canteen of water.

Just over the hill is where our boys had jumped off. Here the visible effects of the enemy's counter-barrage were easily noticed. It must have been more terrible than we had thought. The fire from our own artillery was so deafening that we scarcely noticed that of the Germans, even when it was directed to our section of the front. Out here was evidence a-plenty of its violence. Shell holes were thick, and here or there was a rifle or pack, mute evidence of a man wounded.

There were several dead, too, the victims of that blasting fire. The first dead man I saw was a Mexican Sergeant, from the 2nd Battalion. I crossed the little valley and came to the 2nd battalion P.C. and the first aid station. There was nothing to be done there, so I went on in the direction of the Grand Carre Farm. On my way I saw several more dead Americans. Already someone, probably a first-aid man, had stuck up his rifle, bayonet-end in the ground, as a mark.

I finally arrived at the old farm house, which had been shelled heavily. It was here that I first struck the German front line positions. Along the front as it had been that morning was body after body of German soldiers. Most of them were killed by shell fire—our barrage, but a few of them, I noticed had died from our Infantry. They had stuck by their machine guns until the very last. And in many a machine gun pit was the body of its last defender.

As I passed one of these bodies I noticed a set of German field glasses. On the St.Mihiel front I had been several times in need of field glasses, as Germans respect no one, not even the dead, or those burying those dead. Consequently we had been greatly hampered in our search for the dead, especially in open areas, so I had determined to salvage a pair of glasses at the first opportunity. Equipment of all kinds was scattered around; and then later in the day the opportunity of securing glasses was several times repeated.

Our men were on the next hill, and beyond that hill, on the next one, where Germans, with their machine guns and artillery, were. There was spasmodic machine gun firing at frequent intervals. One battery of 77's was in constant action. They were evidently so well concealed that our artillery observers had not been able to locate them. They had direct observation on our men and dealt us a lot of misery. As I started down the hill, behind our advanced positions, several 77's and whizz-bangs came near me, and I dropped into a shell-hole. After a time, I worked my way down into the valley, where I found the first-aid station of the 3rd Battalion P.C.

Soon after my arrival here, I met Captain Thompson, of the Machine Gun Company, 360th Infantry. I asked him if his company had suffered many casualties. He said "No," but told me where a few of his wounded were still uncared for. Four of us got litters and went and brought them in. The last two were down by a narrow gauge railway in an opening in the valley, almost around the point of the hill. Shells were falling here all the time, the area shifting from time to time. Afterwards we carried in two wounded Germans. Then we went in after another wounded German back toward the farm house. This man had been severely wounded by infantry fire. And he had made several efforts to come down to the aid-station. The enemy artillery had fired on those who attempted to bring him in. Of course, we did not expect to have any pity for ourselves, but the beasts were firing on their own wounded. He was crazy for water, and emptied my canteen without taking it from his lips. We had to carry him in a blanket, and as he was badly wounded, it was rough going for him. He was wounded three times, once being in the right lung.

About the middle of the afternoon I met Nelson, the man who prophesied the war would end September 6, but here it was Nov. 1, and the war was still going full tilt. He was in the first-aid station and had been giving first-aid treatment in the neck of the woods about 300 yards to the left and slightly behind the front. He was now looking for litter bearers to help him get some of these wounded to the aid-station. I went with him, or ahead of him, rather, for he did not then have the desired numbers. I had gone perhaps 75 yards from the first-aid station when the Germans planted two H.E.s near the rock-pit that was the scene of medical treatment. One man who was leaning up against a pile of rocks and dirt was struck in the hip by quite a large fragment. He fell to the ground and arose, twisting fearfully in his pain, crying piteously for help. As he was so near the station and help was at hand, I went on.

It was at this junction that the 1st Battalion went over the top. When they began their advance, the Germans opened up with all they had. During the pause in the advance, the troops suffered heavily from artillery fire. Their only protection was the fox holes which they had hastily dug. Thus for several hours the enemy fired on them at will. But with the renewed attack, it seemed as though a thousand machine guns had opened up to stem the on-coming tide. The vicious rat-a-tat-tat was heard from every direction and front, and a deadly hail swept over the terrain our men had to traverse. At the beginning of the attack, the weird noise of the bullets filled the air above us and occasionally there came a sharp crack that marks the passing of a bullet near at hand. In 15 or 20 minutes the bullets ceased to come over the hill at all. It meant that the attacking party had already passed across the valley and up the opposite slope, probably wiping out the crews that had been operating these guns. I noticed, however, that a very few prisoners passed back to the rear. Perhaps they were sent back another way. Or perhaps no prisoners were taken. Who knows?

I went on toward where the wounded men were said to be. On my way up I passed a dead German who was carrying a type of leather case that was new to me. I examined him more closely and found that the case contained telescopic sights for a sniper. I put the glasses back in the case and was thankful our artillery had silenced forever another German sniper. Soon I reached the wood where the wounded were. "D" Co. and "K" Co. had occupied this wood in the early morning rush, and since that time they had suffered quite heavy casualties from enemy artillery fire. One 75 that was firing on them was visible a short distance in front. It was in a skirt of woods or hedge about half way up the next hill. The gun crew could be seen as they went about their work. One of the Infantry boys, however, finally silenced it.

It was necessary to wait a short time on Nelson, but he soon came with other litter-bearers—four of them. I observed three Germans, who had already received first-aid treatment. There was no hope for the two of them, however, for the pallor of death had already marked their faces, and the eyes of one already had a fixed glassy stare. While we were waiting for something, I don't know what, litter-bearers to be selected perhaps, Nelson told a man that he was to go with the litter. This man answered, "Why don't you make so-and-so go this time? I have already helped with one litter patient." Helped with one litter patient, and it was already past four o'clock! And the other man had not helped with any litter patients. I was thunder-struck as to men quarreling as to which one should go. I wondered how the wounded felt when they heard this discussion. I don't know, but I believe any of them would have changed places with any of the disputants and have done it gladly. In every line of work and under the most pressing need of pain and suffering, there are some who cannot measure up to the standard of the real man, but fall ingloriously short of that ideal. I settled the dispute by giving one of them my place, and asking for walking wounded. I don't remember their names and don't think I would know their faces again; it was my only time to see them, and they were covered with beard of several days' growth. But the memory of their dead will remain with me always. But to the glory of the medical corps, as a whole, be it said that these two were among the exceptions. The medical men have the most human hearts and the most inhuman work of war. They are the type of the Good Samaritan, succoring friend and foe alike, and among their number they have some of the bravest and most unselfish officers and men to be found in our whole forces.

The greater part of the men were so badly wounded that they could scarcely walk. Finally one of them said he believed he could walk by supporting himself on my shoulder. His name was Hooper of Co. "D" and he came from Brownwood, Texas. Only the fear that he might possibly have to remain there all night induced him to attempt the long walk to the ambulance station. But he had been wounded since 11 a.m., and now it was getting toward 5 in the afternoon. He and several others had been without water for several hours, and were quite thirsty. They emptied my canteen, which I had refilled, but that even was not enough for five or six wounded men. It seems that wounded men almost instantly become feverish; at any rate, they want lots of water. Hooper was wounded by shrapnel in five different places. None of the wounds was very serious; but the physical exhaustion and the shock had greatly weakened him. Consequently we made extremely slow progress. He was as gritty and nervy as he could be, and never whimpered nor groaned the least bit. But he simply had to rest occasionally. There is a point beyond which abused and outraged nature will not go, and Hooper had reached that point. He had used up all his reserved power, and had nothing more to fall back on. He was a heavy man, too, over six feet tall and weighing a hundred and eighty pounds. One of the pieces of shrapnel had gone clear through his foot. He could scarcely put any weight on that foot. Another piece of shrapnel had wounded him in both hips, only to a shallow depth to be sure, but enough to interfere with walking.

The machine gun fire ceased by this time, and the artillery fire on both sides had greatly diminished. I wondered how many of the 1st Battalion boys had been killed or wounded in the last advance, but it was too late to find out now. Besides, it was a good mile to the aid station, and Hooper was weak. Just as we crossed the valley and started up the hill toward the Grand Carre Farm building, darkness settled down on us. I did not know exactly where the ambulances were loaded. But we proceeded, and it was easy enough, under the circumstances, to get lost. To make matters worse, two 155's began shelling our vicinity. It was too dark for observation; so I am sure it was only a coincidence. But one shell would fall about 100 yards behind us, and the other about the same distance in front. We were following a rather dim road or trail and the Germans were evidently shelling it on the assumption that it would be used in bringing up men, artillery, or rations. But they guessed wrong, for Hooper and I were the only human beings in sight. We were afraid to stop, and, in spite of his weakened condition, kept pottering on. But the good Lord was with us once more, and we escaped injury. Our journey led us down a ravine, in which there were some good fox-holes. As the shelling was getting nearer, closing in on us, as it were, in scissors fashion, and as Hooper was too exhausted to go any further, and also as I knew we were lost, we turned into one of these holes. I made Hooper as comfortable as I could on some blankets that I found in two discarded packs. We had not been in this shelter more than a minute when we both saw a shell hit squarely in the path about 50 yards ahead. Both is us agreed that it would have gotten us. It could hardly have missed us, as we would just about have had time to be there. What made us turn in? I don't know positively; it may have been only an accident, but I am inclined to think that it was that Higher Power, whose eye sees even the fall of the sparrow. While we were waiting here for the shelling to stop, or pass on, a dud came over, and went into the ground only a few feet away. We could hear it sizzling and frying as the hot metal came into contact with the damp earth. And it is the same kind of metal that passed through human flesh.

Pretty soon I started out to find the aid station from which the wounded were evacuated to hospital. I finally came out on the road running Northwest of Bantheville. I finally came out into the right road after much turning, twisting and stumbling. I have seen many roads congested with traffic, but this beyond the possibility of a doubt was the worst. It was the mad, feverish effort to get artillery, men, and supplies of rations and ammunition up to the ever-advancing front. Vehicles of all kinds were in this jam. Most noticeable of all, perhaps, were the large caterpillar tractors which were bringing up the large six-inch artillery. This heavy artillery was being placed along the right bank of the road, and frequently was the cause of the stopping of all traffic. Mule teams loaded with ammunition, or rations, were intermingled here and there. Heavy trucks, Ford trucks, Ford passenger cars, and staff cars from different headquarters, were lined up indiscriminately, one behind the other. Ambulances negotiated the jam the quickest, undoubtedly because of the willingness to give the first passage to the wounded. Motor dispatch riders also wound through it quickly. But for any other kind of vehicle a long wait was necessary.

At last I arrived at the first-aid station, and soon four of us started back with a litter for Hooper. The men who went with me went willingly, but they were tired out, almost to the point of exhaustion by the heavy demands of the day's work. We rested frequently, though, and finally Hooper was at the aid station, tagged, and waiting for the ambulance. I left him with about 40 others, all waiting for ambulances that carried only four litters at one time, and every trip through that frightfully congested road. The groans from suffering and shivering men was something I can never forget. The pain was bad enough, but the cold, with their low physical condition, greatly increased their agony. One poor fellow kept crying that his foot was cold. I covered him up the best I could, but he was still crying as long as I could hear him.

As though to increase my day's work, I got lost again. It was so dark now, with the mist falling, too, that I could not follow a straight line. After about an hour, I wandered back to the road, and went through Bantheville to the P.C. We had opened a can of corn willy in a shell hole where Hooper and I stopped; so I was not very hungry, and I turned in at once.

Nov. 2

We were told early this morning that the 1st Battalion, in their attack yesterday afternoon, took Andevanne and Hill 243. Hill 243 was gained about 8 o'clock. I would like to know about their casualties but nothing definite had been reported.

Chaplain Lewis told me to wait for a detail of eight men that would go with me to bury the dead in a certain area behind us. The detail did not show up. But two or three of us searched over the area for some of the 32nd Division's dead. The lieutenant who we had noticed on our way to the front had been buried, and so had others near him. A burial detail from the 89th Division was at work in this area, and they had buried most of the dead. We found quite a few dead Germans, but we decided to leave them for later arrivals, as our own dead needed our attention first. However, we hurriedly buried five of them in machine gun pits.

Nov. 3

Everyone was down-cast this morning by the news that the 1st Battalion in the evening before had been almost wiped out. The report was that only three line-officers were left unwounded, and Capt. Delario was known to have been killed, with perhaps other officers. The Colonel gathered all the staff officers and those on special duty at Regimental Headquarters together just before all of them started toward the front. He said that every one of them should encourage and cheer both men and officers. I am afraid it was hard work. It is not easy to pull the wool over men's eyes on the battle front. Besides the effort to conceal or minimize the real situation, if it is known and evident to all, sounds hollow and insincere.

As it had been reported that wounded lay out on the field all night with no one to carry them to the aid station, a party was organized under Chaplain Lewis and Lt. Bartlett to search for and carry in the wounded. I wanted to go, but the Colonel had already told Chaplain Lewis that he should go. So that left me to help with the burying. I regret exceedingly that I did not stay up at the front, until our regiment should be relieved. The wounded are much more in need of attention than the dead. In any future fighting I shall manage to be at the front. We buried 15 Americans today.

Nov. 4

Chaplain Lewis returned late last night, and his report of the situation is grim enough. However, the German resistance seems to have been broken at this point, as the 179th Brigade, which relieved the 180th yesterday morning, advanced yesterday with little opposition. Already the front was so far advanced that no small arms firing could be heard. The 360th is pretty badly done up. No one seems to know how the 359th on our right has suffered.

My detail and I buried 11 Americans and four Germans today. Most of the time was spent in searching for bodies. We cleaned up a section of the Bois-de-Bantheville, and found quite a few men belonging to other divisions. Apparently they had been dead for some time. Most of them were killed by machine gun fire. One of the men had fifty-six dollars in American money on his person. Some of the bodies were rather badly decomposed. Off one of those badly decomposed bodies, in searching for personal effects, was taken a pencil. A wanderer (?) from some medical detachment of another division, or perhaps with the balloon (?) organization was standing near and I asked if anyone needed a pencil. I did not think anyone would take the pencil, as I had seen no one before who would take anything from the body of a dead American, although they were willing enough to rifle the pockets of a dead German. This man answered, "Yes, I would like it as a souvenir." Several of us were surprised and angered. For my own part I felt like trying a stiff punch on his jaw, but I decided that such a man could not get the viewpoint of the rest of us. Several of the men in the detail said afterwards that it would do them good to tie up with him. He is the first of his type that I have met, and I hope he is the last.

Food is becoming an extremely serious matter; all the 360th kitchens have moved to the front, and, of course, we can't get chow from them. Other kitchens have strict orders not to feed stragglers, or men belonging to any other organization. So we are left standing high and dry. Today Sgt. Placke of the 2nd Bn. and I went to Romagne, but we were able to get nothing. When we came back to Bantheville, we met Lt. Pate of the supply company who said he would bring us a little to get along on. He may come tomorrow. It's easy for a detail like ours to be forgotten. We made the best of the situation and salvaged some corn willy and some hard tack. A Jew in "D" Co's detail managed to get a can of butter from some place or other. No one knows how he got it, and he is mysterious enough to keep it to himself. However, we do not care. So we managed to make a fairly good meal.

Nov. 5

We moved up today and have fairly good quarters in Andevanne. We are sleeping on German beds and I am sure that we shall all get the cooties. So far I have been lucky enough to miss them. It fell to our lot today to bury a bunch of men out of the 359th, who had been killed almost in the edge of Bantheville. We also buried one German, who was in a terrible stage of decomposition. He had been wounded and carried to an aid station. It seemed that after his wounds had received attention, another shell came and killed him, covering him with the wreckage of the building. As it was late, we put him into a shell hole and hurriedly threw a little dirt over him. It is a wonder we ever found him at all.

**Regimental
Post Command
at Andevanne**

Church at Andevanne

**Aid Station,
Andevanne**

Main street of Villers-devant-Dun

German ammunition on Hill 243 near Villers-devant-Dun, 77s

YMCA at Villers-devant-Dun

Grave of two
American officers
and twenty-five men,
Villers-devant-Dun

Only house left
standing in
Montfaucon,
used as a "Y"

Remains of
church in
Montfaucon

Church at Romagne

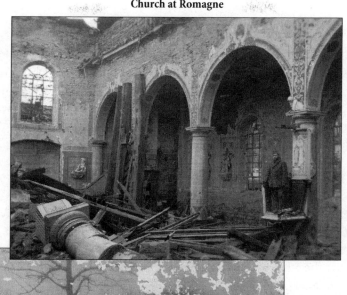

32nd Division
cemetery at Nantillois

Road leading
from Sassey
to Mouzay

Nov. 6

Both burial details worked together today, and they got along faster. Chaplain Lewis, with part of the Detail, searched out and brought in the bodies to a place near the Grand Carre farm house. I stayed at the graves, getting the names and personal effects of each of the dead men. Among the bodies brought in was that of Tom Lambertson. I did not know that he had been killed. I knew him in the Depot Brigade and had heard him speak often of his mother and sisters. Altogether we buried 28, and have a few more yet.

Four men out of the detail and I buried three men out the 353rd Infantry, of the 89th Division, who were killed by machine gun fire not a hundred yards from the last edge of the Argonne Forest. The enemy had one of the few lanes that are found in these thick forests covered with machine guns. As these men came into this opening they were killed, one after the other, and fell, one on each other. Their death was doubtless typical of many who died in that forest. We enlarged the fox hole and laid them side by side.

Nov. 7

We buried all the bodies that we could find in the immediate vicinity of the farm house and crossed over to the next hill, just south of Andevanne. Thirty-two were buried in this grave at the old farm house. This morning another man, whom I met in the Depot Brigade, was brought to the graves. His name was Charlie Barden, and he was a fine chap. His father is a Methodist minister, near Goliad, Texas.

On the next hill is where the 1st Battalion jumped off on the afternoon of November 1. It was a veritable shambles, all those who were killed in this particular sector met death from a galling artillery fire. The mutilation and mangling was something terrible. As we left the Grand Carre farm we passed a piece of human flesh about twice as large as a man's hand. We searched and searched for any other portion of the unfortunate soldier, but nothing else could be found. We picked it up on a shovel, dropped it into a shell hole and covered it up. On the next hill we found one man only the legs from the knees down. Evidently a shell made a direct hit on him. Not another bit of his body could be found. Although shreds of flesh were scattered here and there, already black from decomposition. Fortunately his tags were near, and we were able to establish his identity. He belonged to the 3rd Battalion. And others, also, were torn and horribly mangled. In a terribly shocking manner, they were. One body had the intestine laying exposed; another had the head split open by a large shell fragment; another had part of his face shot away in a sickening terrible manner.

And this is the glory and the glamour of war; this is the price of victory; this is the sacrifice that is always demanded by the devotees of wars. It is a thrilling and sublime sight to see men advancing coolly into the jaws of death, facing the screeching shells with unflinching nerve, and going forward over a bullet swept plain. But the thrill and the sublimity come as a result of war, and are not war itself. As Donnel Hankey says in "A Student in Arms," men act a glorious part in war because they are men, and not because war itself is glorious. There is nothing glorious in war. It is beastly and brutish. What had these men done that they should be deprived of life in this violent manner, away from relatives and friends, and in a distant, alien land? They went to their death with a smile and a jest; but human life and human rights should be so sacred and inviolable as to be safe and secure to every individual in every land. On the other hand, what punishment can be sufficient and just for the men who cause war? A terrible price has to be paid in the lives of men on the battlefield, and all humanity is deprived of the potential benefits of their work. How can a fitting penalty commensurate with the crime be meted out to these men? Some day all men must face a universal court of justice, and I believe that the heaviest sentences will be given those who caused or promoted war. It will be at least just; for they are the cause of the world's heaviest loss of life, and also of all that endless suffering which follows in the train of war.

Among some letters on one of the dead, we found a picture of his wife and child, an infant about six months old. The picture was so full of expression and so clear and life-like that almost involuntarily each one of us hurriedly passed it on as we thought of the fate of the husband and the father lying cold and stiff at our feet. Many sad and wistful ears will wait, but will never hear the approach of men who went to war. When the boys return there will be tears in some eyes, because all will not return. It is another of the glories of war, that it makes widows and orphans.

Nov. 8

We continued our work as usual. It is getting to be trying to our nerves, and everyone is anxious to be through with this job. It is work that must be done, but no one desires to do it. News from the front is extremely scarce. There is not much artillery firing that we can hear. There has been quite an advance, and they are probably waiting for artillery and supplies. We buried 31 Germans today.

Nov. 9

We continued our work even more anxiously today. We thought we could finish. But so much of our time was spent in searching over a large area that it will take at least another day. Chaplain Lewis says that he has dreamed several nights now about dead men. Last night was my first time. This work is hard on all of us, and I believe it would eventually run a man crazy. Several of the men, as Sanford of "A" Co., say that every time they start to eat they think of the dead men and that sickening odor comes up, and they can't eat.

The 3rd Bn., and also the Machine Gun Co., came in today. I saw John Arthur for a few minutes. He had pulled through all right. I was uneasy about him, but it seems that the machine gun company had suffered only light losses in comparison with the rifle companies.

We are shut off from the world, marooned and isolated; we have not been able to get any news in about a week now. Today an M.P. did tell us that there was a rumor to the effect that Germany had asked for an armistice. But the rumor is unconfirmed, and I am afraid it is like all those rumors we heard at Domgermain.

Nov. 10

At last we have finished our work, and tomorrow we shall go back to our organizations. It took us all day, and hard work at that. Again today most of the time was spent in searching for bodies. Our total for the day was two Americans and eight Germans. Altogether on this work, my detail and I have buried 101 Americans and about 70 Germans; and Chaplain Lewis and his detail have buried just about the same number. One of the Americans buried today was an 80th Division man. He had apparently gone back for water, as he had 13 big French canteens slung on his shoulder. He was killed in the outskirts of Andevanne, and we buried him in the cemetery. A peculiar thing about his death was that there were no marks of violence on his body. A gas shell must have exploded right by him.

Last night somewhere about midnight, the 360th got orders to move up to the front again. Every man of them was so worn out that I don't see how they can do any more fighting until they have had a rest, and replacements. They had about 15 kilometers to make today.

All of us here are so hopeful tonight that we are almost happy. German commissioners have actually come across to see Gen. Foch about an armistice. That much at least we know to be true, even in our isolation. We are fervently praying that it may mean the end; it is too terrible to kill men in such a murderous business. This detail work behind the lines, following up the battle, is even worse. It is enough to drive a man crazy, or to make him absolutely heartless or indifferent about men. God give us peace.

Nov. 11

At last it is over. The fighting is finished, and there will be no more slaughter, in this war at least. We had eaten all the reserved rations we could find at Andevanne, and left there at 3:30 for our organizations. At the edge of the village, near the cemetery, an M.P., who was directing traffic, told us that he had just been told by a truck driver that an armistice had been arranged. He did not know about the time it was to go into effect, though. We could hardly believe that it was true, but we were delighted, and started out on the long hike with light hearts. When we came to the edge of Villers-devant-Dun another M.P., stationed where the road forked—and one road went to Andevanne and the other to Aincreville—said that hostilities were to cease at 11:00 o'clock. He had just heard it from Division Headquarters, which, at this time, was at Villers-devant-Dun.

We could hardly realize that it was true. There was no cheering, or yelling, although there were over fifty of us in the detail. One or two tried to holler, but only a feeble sound was heard. We couldn't say anything that would do justice to the occasion. Our hearts came up into our throats from sheer joy and choked all utterance. But every face showed faintly, but unmistakably pleasure and the eyes spoke volumes where lips could not mutter a word. We contentedly eased our packs on our shoulders, shifting our weight into a comfortable position, and eagerly listened to the meager details. No speaker ever had more willing listeners. Was the war about to stop? We could hardly believe it. We could not grasp its tremendous meaning. And we listened, with visions of peace already in our hearts. It had been extremely foggy when we left Andevanne, and was still quite foggy, although not nearly so dense. While we were hearing the news the sun almost broke through strong enough to make the ice on the leaves and branches standing the forks of the road glitter and twinkle in its light. In spite of the fog, the mud, and the cold, and the long march ahead of us we were happier than we had been in many a day.

Chaplain Lewis and I went on down to Division Headquarters to make our report. As we were passing through the sloppy street, several inches deep in mud and slush, a lieutenant, just back from the front, came out of a house. We had heard two shots when we were at the forks of the road and wondered what it meant. We now learned. This lieutenant was so happy that when he learned of the armistice in true western style he discharged his revolver twice in the air.

We went on down to Headquarters, and found Chaplain Reese, and reported. He was as glad as any of the rest of us, and happier, because he had just heard more news and details of the armistice. Germany was to be compelled to give up so much of her war materiel that she would not have a chance to ever come back. He gathered a few officers and men together and held a short thanksgiving service. There was only a prayer, and a song, "My Country 'Tis of Thee." Length is not always essential to earnestness.

Chaplain Reese had just received a wire from G.H.Q., saying that my application for a chaplaincy required another recommendation. I thought a commission did not make any difference, now that the war was over. Chaplain Lewis, however, dictated one and signed one, just a short hour before the armistice went into effect.

We went back to the detail, told them what we had learned, and started once more for the front. We got lost and walked several kilometers out of the way; but what did that matter. We did not have anything to eat for dinner and were told to pass on when we stopped at Division ration dump. We also passed up some artillery kitchens near Dun-sur-Meuse. We knew that we could not get any rations there.

Did we howl about it, and was there any cursing? Not a bit. We were sitting on the top side of the world and did not care how things wagged. We saw Dun-sur-Meuse, crossed the Meuse at Sassey, and finally made

Mouzay. The sun came out just a little while this afternoon, but gave almost a ghostly appearance to the country. Even nature was making an effort at rejoicing over the return of peace. We had anxiously listened at 11 o'clock to see whether the armistice was a fake or was really true. At ten minutes until 11 you could hear quite a bit of firing; but after 11 not a report was heard. At any rate, the fighting was over, and we would have a good chance of getting back home. Germany had been whipped and whipped good. For this reason we did not feel tired when we reached our journey's end. Just before we reached Mouzay we had to pass through that part of the Meuse valley which the Germans flooded. There was little evidence of fighting. Only a few dead horses, a shell hole now and then, or a tree scarred by fragments of shells. But all of the bridges over the canal by the roadside had been blown up, and the big trees all cut down, to dam the water up to hinder our advance. It all came too late, however.

We are in Mouzay tonight, and already war seems to be miles and miles away. The kitchens are still at work, feeding late arrivals, and messengers come and go with all the haste of war. But with what a difference! The cars and motorcycles were glaring their headlights, lighting roads ahead of them. This is a luxury they have not enjoyed since they first came to the front. The houses are all fixed up, and the windows do not have to be camouflaged in dread of an aerial attack. The main street here with all its lights and cars is almost like an American town.

Thank God! The war is over—actually, if not formally. No more hardship or hunger, or night marches! No more "going over the top" or hiding in "fox-holes" from the ominous shell or the machine gun bullet. No more wounded passing to the rear, walking or on stretchers, mortally wounded or maimed or disfigured for life. No more laying of men wrapped in a blanket in a scooped out shell hole or hastily dug grave. Thank God, the terrible destruction of life is at last a thing of the past for us! And thank Him again because victory, with the forces of right and freedom, a crushing defeat has been administered to militarism. Might has been overcome by might and Right is justified once more.

The Letters to Myrtle Arthur

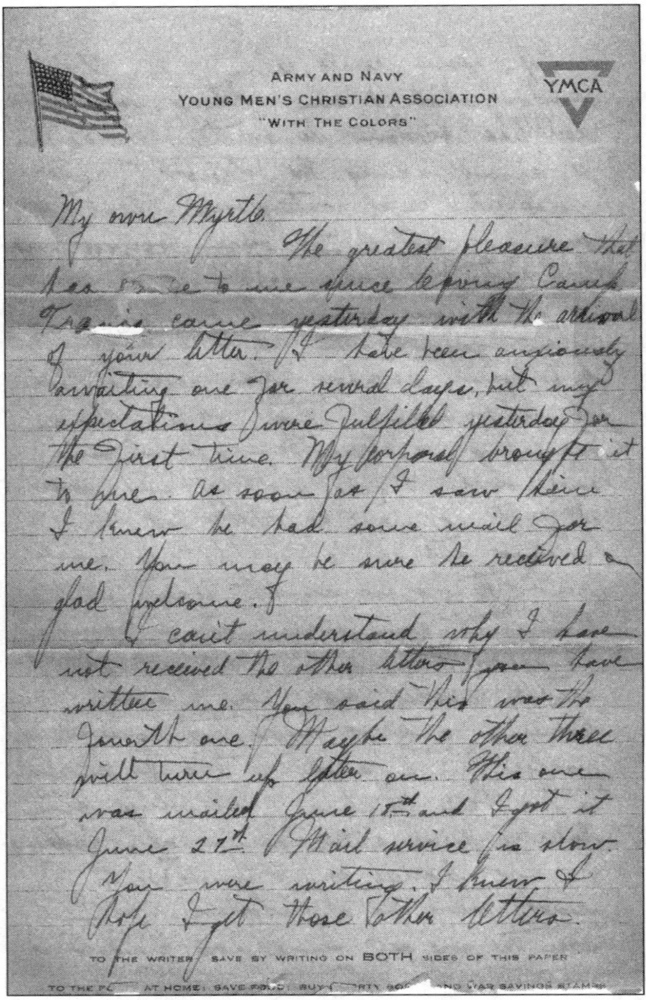
ARMY AND NAVY
YOUNG MEN'S CHRISTIAN ASSOCIATION
"WITH THE COLORS"
YMCA

My own Myrtle,

The greatest pleasure that has come to me since leaving Camp Travis came yesterday with the arrival of your letter. I have been anxiously awaiting one for several days, but my expectations were fulfilled yesterday for the first time. My corporal brought it to me. As soon as I saw him I knew he had some mail for me. You may be sure he received a glad welcome.

I can't understand why I have not received the other letters you have written me. You said this was the fourth one. Maybe the other three will turn up later on. This one was mailed June 10th and I got it June 27th. Mail service is slow. You were writing, I know. I hope I get those other letters.

TO THE WRITER: SAVE BY WRITING ON BOTH SIDES OF THIS PAPER
TO THE F[illegible] AT HOME: SAVE FOOD; BUY [illegible] AND WAR SAVINGS STAMPS

May 1918—June 1919

Letter 1a: May 19, 1918
San Antonio, Texas
[Envelope:] Found in street

My dearest Myrtle,

I suppose you think I have forgotten but that is far from the truth. The main reason why I have not written is that I have been busy. They are putting us through these days. We get up at six o'clock. From then until eleven-thirty, we are at Uncle Sam's service—and believe me, he uses them every minute of that time. We drill most of the time. The first thing we do, though after breakfast is to police up barracks and grounds. At seven-forty five we begin drilling. It usually takes from eleven-thirty until [?] to wash and dust up. We finish dinner and then a little rest before one o'clock. Then we drill until four-thirty. An hour is given for retreat. That is, to make preparations for retreat. After retreat comes supper. Even supper is not the final act in the day's tragedy, because some of us have to go to the school for noncommissioned officers from seven until nine, except on holidays. So you can see that I do not have much time that I can call my own.

Saturday afternoon is a half holiday. Most of the boys are going to town this afternoon. They can get passes lasting until eleven o'clock. I went to town last Wednesday. So I don't feel under the necessity of going again today.

The new men who have been transferred into old organizations are having all laid on them that they can bear. Today a lot of them were started on a twenty two mile hike to the target range. Some of them will undoubtedly fall out. The ambulance can pick them up if they are not 'faking.' A lot of them have already been returned to our company because they were unable to make good in the companies to which they were assigned. They were either 'boobs' or weaklings. Some of these poor fellows will never make anything more glorious than k. p. I feel sorry for them.

Speaking of k.p., I am reminded that I was on k.p. last Wednesday. I was on from twelve-thirty until about eight that night. That was my first time and I could live happily if I knew it was my last time. I am in hopes that it is. It is easy for me to see now why ladies hate dish washing. I'll never laugh at anyone again when they are finished with washing dishes.

I have been promoted now. I am a second class private. So be careful how you address me. It would be an unpardonable breach of etiquette to address me as "Recruit" when I am "Private" etc.

I am expecting to be made a corporal when this next increment comes in. Some of us are to be made corporals and I am hoping that I shall be one of the lucky ones. I am getting more drilling than anyone else in our company. That suits me fine. Also I am studying drill regulations.

I am not to be transferred. They have made me a part of the permanent nucleus of the 65th Co. That means that I am stuck here permanently unless I can make the officers' training camp.

You don't know how much suspense I have been in this week. There was exactly one week that I did not hear from you. It was not your fault either. But that didn't change the situation at all. I thought something had come up that had resulted in my losing your love. I know now that it was senseless, but during two or three days it was a very painful feeling. I came to realize then, as I never had before, how much you and your love mean to me. I had made up my mind to write you a very "appealing" letter this afternoon. But fortunately I got both your cards yesterday afternoon. One of them had meandered around by Camp Bowie. It reassured me fully, though, to read them. I knew that you still loved me. I will write you a good letter tomorrow, if I am capable of such a thing. I want to get this one to town this afternoon and you will get it tomorrow.

I am scheduled to make a talk at the Y.M.C.A. tomorrow morning. Some old stuff will fill the bill. I haven't time for anything new.

Aren't you glad school is out? You will be entirely free by next Monday or Tuesday. I am glad for you. You deserve a vacation now.

Love me lots for all my love is yours.

Eugene

Letter 4: undated
Wednesday morning

My dearest Myrtle,

I am on guard duty today and during my hours off I am going to try to write you. I don't know whether it is exactly in accordance with regulations or not. Nothing has been said about it at all. If I don't write now, I won't have another opportunity until tonight.

Our company is doing all the military police work here in Camp Travis. I am afraid we are permanent here. I came on for the first time yesterday afternoon at seven o'clock. I don't mind doing guard duty, but I would much prefer guarding Germans to standing guard over Americans. If I am going to shoot anyone, I want it to be Germans.

We are on duty at what is called the stockade. Prisoners are kept here, not prisoners of war, but men who have violated army regulations. Usually they are rather serious offenders too. The stockade is surrounded by a high barb wire fence and it is closely guarded at all times.

Guarding the stockade and guarding prisoners is a very respectable duty. I did not know there was so much to it. If a guard allows a prisoner to escape, he takes the prisoner's place and also receives his sentence. Isn't that hard? So, as much fellow feeling as I may have for the prisoners here, not one of them is going to put me in as his substitute. I would hate to shoot a man, but since, if the situation arises, I am wholly responsible for them, I shall not hesitate one moment. Do you think I would shoot? I might do as you did that night on the back porch. I hope though that the emergency will never present itself.

We are not allowed to communicate with the prisoners. At times that is hard to carry out. A new guard from our company yesterday let a prisoner escape and now the guard is a prisoner. I knew him before he went on guard and have known him by sight for several weeks. He is only a kid and I expect he became so excited that he could not use his gun. I wanted so much to speak to him, and I had an excellent opportunity at one time. But you can bet that I am not going to break that regulation either in letter or in spirit. It won't do them any good and it might do me a lot of harm.

Guarding is lonely work, especially at night. It increases my resentment against the Germans. Honest people want to be in bed, except on special occasions, by midnight. One of my times on duty was from one-thirty to three-thirty. Can you imagine anything more delightful? A heavy rain falling at the same time might add the finishing touch. My wrath against the Germans increases every day. I'll be glad when I can unload some of it off on them. It will do me a lot of good, whether it materially injures them or not.

I am determined to go across at the first opportunity. Furthermore, I am going to do all I can to make the opportunity. I don't know whether there is any chance or not. But I can't believe that I am going to be 'stuck,' literally and figuratively, here for the duration of the war.

Yesterday morning I saw one of the prettiest sights my eyes have ever witnessed. The 359th and the 360th regiments, with their respective regimental bands, were out on the drill field for drill and later a review. I never before realized how good soldiers our boys can be. They were marching in columns about thirty abreast. They were a machine. Some of the best drilled units were practically faultless. The men moved as one man. Right foot and left hand, or left foot, would swing forward across the whole front in perfect unison. And the best part about it is that some of those boys have been in their units only three or four weeks. When I saw them and heard the music. I felt that I just must go. I never before realized the importance of music in war. When those martial strains come floating through the air, it is hard not to march. Of course, I naturally notice any religious 'overtones'[?]; and two of the pieces they played were "How Firm a Foundation" and "Onward, Christian Soldiers." It may have been just a happen-so, and doubtless was, but it seemed to me to be a fit expression of the trust and the cause of our people. Our armies are going to give a glorious account of themselves. My greatest wish for myself is that I was going over shortly too. Yes, I had noticed where Jim Ward was severely wounded. A Mississippi boy that I knew well, was also in the casualty list a few days ago. Indeed, it is coming home to us. That is what makes me so anxious to go over. Not to get wounded, but to be with friends who are already in the struggle.

But let's change the subject so far I have written of nothing but war.

. . .

It almost makes my heart sick, when I think about it, that we have not had that opportunity to talk over the future at all in relation to us two. That ought to be one of the sweetest parts of a couple's life, to plan for the future they are to spend together. We shall have to charge this up to the war, as we do so many other things. But if God wills it, we shall have this pleasure after the war. We shall know each other better and our love will be many times stronger because of the separation.

Precious, I expect I shall be unusually busy from now on. "Intensive training" is to be given to our company according to the latest order. So if I can't write long letters, you will know the reason why. But you continue to write me just as these last letters have been—long and sweet. They mean more to me than all the other letters I get.

Remember that I love you with all my heart and am waiting for the day when we shall be together not to be separated.

Your own,

Eugene.

Letter 5: undated

My own dearest Myrtle,

Only a few minutes remain until the bugle will blow "Lights out." But I am so lonely for you that I am going to write a little while anyway. It is impossible for us to be together so we have to take the best substitute which is sending our thoughts by letter. It is a poor substitute, though, at times. A letter can't bring your smile or the sound of your voice.

. . .

Does the tone of my letters impress you as despondent or dissatisfied? It certainly is not my intention that you should gain such an impression. I may grumble and growl. That is a soldier's privilege. But, as we were drilling today out on the prairie under a hot sun. I asked myself suddenly if I had any regret for having come into the army. I am glad and thankful that I am able to say there is not now and hasn't been a single one. I am keenly disappointed at having to stay here in Camp Travis and even more at being stuck on M.P. but if I can't get anywhere else, I'll go on here without a complaint. I am afraid that I may at times say things that give the impression that I am dissatisfied and would like to get out. I do want to get out — when the war is over, but not until then. My complaint is against the war, and not against my work at Camp Travis. So bear this in mind when you hear me saying things about army life.

You would be surprised if you knew how often I think of you. Even in our formations and our drills you are constantly in my mind. My thoughts are always turning to you.

. . .

Friday Evening—

. . .

This morning was the hardest drilling that we have had since I came here. We drilled all the morning with our guns. They weigh only a fraction over nine pounds, but they get heavy after carrying them for several hours. We were drilling from eight until eleven-thirty. Usually we have a conference period of about forty-five minutes between ten and eleven o'clock, but it has been dispensed with. I, for one, am glad of it. They were usually dry and soporific. You ask me how I like to drill these hot days. I don't think it is so bad. I like a drill such as we had this morning. That is the only kind that does any good. I don't notice the heat very much as long as we are drilling and in the open. As soon as we get out of the wind, the heat becomes uncomfortable.

Some of the boys told me that the 360th left yesterday. I was up there night before last and they were ready then. John said he was sure they would leave yesterday. I hated to see them go. I know more boys in that regiment than in any other. John was anxious to go. He said that the nearer the time came, the more impatient he became for their departure. I am glad that he feels that way about it. He was feeling unusually lighthearted when I saw him last. He has more life about him than I ever thought he had.

. . .

Haven't the Americans been doing some fine work in France? It wasn't on a large scale, of course, but it shows what Americans can do. I'll be glad when we have a really large army over there. Maybe this affair could soon be ended.

. . .

I must close. This is too long already. Remember that I love with all my love and heart, dearest darling, and that I am living for our future my life and my love.

Yours forever,

Eugene

Letter 6: June 1918

My dearest Myrtle,

Isn't this a beautiful Sunday morning? I had planned to go into town to church, but my plans are easily changed when representatives of Uncle Sam have other uses for me. At present, I am 'sticking around' with nothing to do. I wanted to go to the Y.M.C.A. but I am afraid even that far off. A Y.M.C.A. man came up here not five minutes ago to ask me to lead his service this morning. It was ten-thirty-five there. I would have attended it, if I could have left here.

The men are leaving here fast. In a few days more the whole ninetieth division will be gone. The depot brigade will stay on, of course. That's the luck of men in it. But the others are on their way. The old place looks rather deserted and lonely. Everything is quiet and still now. The contrast between the stir of the last few days and the silence and absence of men now is almost painful. But it won't be too long until a lot of new men will be sent in, if reports are to be credited.

I have had another turn at M.P. work. It is more distasteful to me now than ever. I despise to have to guard prisoners in the U.S. It would be an entirely different question in France. It would be a lot easier over there.

Did you know we had a lot of Mennonites in Camp? Forty one more sent to prison Friday afternoon. They are a sect which refuses to serve in even a non-combatant breech. At first they were willing to do certain kinds of work, but now they don't and wouldn't do a thing. Some of them have turned out their beards and, believe me, they have the appearance of a grizzly bear. They are awaiting sentence now. A sergeant who has had them in charge all along said he thought they would each get twenty years at Leavenworth. It is severe, unless they are doing it to get out of the war altogether. I can approve their stand it if is adherence to convictions of conscience, although I am convinced that they are mistaken.

Good news came to me this morning. It is almost certain that I shall be transferred to an overseas organization. I have been trying all this week, but I had no luck. Last night I tried harder than ever before and I had given up entirely. I lay awake a long time thinking about a transfer and you. Only two "avenues of escape" were left me. But this morning before breakfast, the top sergeant called me and asked me if I still wanted to go. A memorandum had come down requesting the names of Class A men available for transfer. He said he would see the company commander and try to get my name sent in. He spoke to the commander, but the commander sent back on the memorandum that he could not spare any "A" men. But the sergeant said, as he passed me, for I was anxiously awaiting the result of their interview, "I am afraid it's all up, Mac, but you might see the lieutenant." After quite a silence, he at last consented and wrote out an order for me and I myself took it to battalion headquarters. I had to do some earnest pleading to get him to send in my name. So now I am waiting to be examined for overseas service. I am expecting to be called at any moment. That is why I am staying so close. It would simply kill me if I should yet lose it on account of my own carelessness.

No one can tell me that God does not take an interest in even the smallest things in one's life. It was just an accident that the sergeant knew that I wanted a transfer. After supper last night I loafed by his window, hardly knowing what to do with myself. I must have shown on my face or by my appearance, that I was looking for something to turn up. At any rate, he asked me to come in and sit a little while. While I was in. I told him how I had tried to get across ever since I went into Y.M.C.A. work and up to the present, but with no apparent success. You can imagine how thankful I was this morning. I know you have seen county prisoners at work on the roads with guards stationed around. That is an excellent picture of M.P. work here in Camp Travis. The prospect of several months of that was more than I could face. I don't know yet what organization I am to be transferred to. Frankly I don't care, just so I get transferred into something that is going across. There are indications, though, that it will be the 315th ammunition supply train. I don't know anything about that branch of the service, but that's a small matter.

What do you think about my trying so hard to get a transfer? At times, it seems just like sticking one's hand into a lion's mouth. But, in a way, I have been doing that ever since I first left Edna. You were to be considered because it means more to you than to anyone else, (unless it is my mother.) But I have heard you say on several occasions that if you were a man you would not be satisfied until you got to France. That is exactly my conviction and desire.

I have had dinner since writing the above and have been helping on a report. It is now two-thirty. No call yet for transfer.

. . .

My darling, you hardly know how much it helps me to know that you are praying for me. You remember that when I left the first time for Camp Travis that you said you would always pray for me. It gives me a feeling of peace and confidence. I am sure that your prayers will be answered. I pray often every day that God will keep us both for each other.

. . .

Your very own,

Eugene

Letter 7: June 9, 1918

My dearest Myrtle,

This has been a busy afternoon with me. It is now four o'clock, and I have been on pins ever since noon. An acting noncom's life is no sinecure, I assure you. He has to see to everything on his floor.

We had two sick men in quarters this afternoon. I thought one of them would die before they came after him. I sent in his name at twelve-thirty. An officer from the hospital was supposed to come over at once and examine him. At least a dozen trips were made before any came through. The sick man had a very high pulse and fever at first, soon followed by a hard chill. I think it was all caused by intense pain. I thought he would go into convulsions. The doctor who examined him did not tell us what his ailment was, but he left here on the run and it wasn't very long until an ambulance from the base hospital arrived. He was evidently very sick, for the ambulance went off very slowly. If a man is not very sick, they break all speed laws. I would like to know how he came out and what is the matter with him.

The other fellow has influenza. I think he is rather putting on. The other fellow was unconscious.

. . .

I know now how much you mean to me. The hardest part of my being in the army is the separation from you. I did not know until lately how you filled my whole life. The loss of no other person would mean as much to me as losing you. The affection of friends and relatives is naturally often broken. But love between a man and a woman is different. It looks more to the future, especially when it is a newly discovered love as ours is. I miss you more and more and I can't be happy again until I am with you. I would like so often to tell you how I love you, but I can't because I can't find adequate words. You know that I love you with all my heart, though, don't you? And that is all we need to know.

. . .

Sixteen of us were told last night that we were to be held here as part of a permanent personnel in quarantine. That means that we may be here for the duration of the war. If it lasts very long, I shall get a transfer. Otherwise, I had just about as soon be at one place as at another. The first sergeant said all of us would be made noncoms. That is, if we make good.

. . .

How are you feeling now? I hope you are entirely well and getting 'fleshy' again. I hope you will get real fat when school is out. You have only two weeks more, haven't you? My, how tempus fugit!

. . .

How I wish I could be with you tonight!
Lots and lots of love—

Eugene.

Sunday Evening

Letter 8: June 10, 1918

My own dearest Myrtle,

This will be only a short letter, I am afraid, as I have several other little notices to write. We are confined to quarters tonight and probably leave tomorrow morning. We don't know positively, but I am sure that it won't be long. I want to write a few little notes to some home folks and friends so that they may know where to call (?) on me.

I could sit down to my writing without worry, if it were not for the fact that I have a lot of washing staring me in the face. You see, I am still doing washing. I washed a lot stuff yesterday afternoon and have almost as much to wash again tonight. I suppose I had just as well get accustomed to it, as it will be necessary for me to do it all when I get in France. It is not a cheering prospect though.

I was transferred again last night. When they told me I was to leave the infirmary, my heart fell to zero, for I thought sure that I was to be returned to the M.P.'s. But it was not such bad luck as that. I am now in Co.B. 315th supply train. It is a branch of the quartermaster's corps and provides the men at the front with food and other needed supplies. We don't [provide] any ammunition to the men though. I am very much disappointed that I could not stay in the medical detachment, but this is not bad at all.

I want to tell you what I did to get your letter today. I know it would be my last one for some time, unless almost a miracle happens. It can happen, though, and maybe I'll get one somewhere sometime soon. My company is in exactly the opposite extremity of the camp from the sixty-fifth company. It is about two miles over there. I asked the sergeant if I could possibly get my mail. He said I had exactly forty-five minutes. I made it by walking, double timing and riding in jitneys, but it was close work. I am going to take this letter with me and keep it as long as I can.

It is rather queer to be returning your letters to you, but it is only as a trust. I shall call for every one of them someday. I am sure that you will make sure that no one sees them when that box comes. What would Ruth [Myrtle's youngest sister] do if she knew the contents of some of them? Keep them for me and we shall read them together at some future time.

. . .

My own Myrtle, you don't know how hard it is not to see you before I go. I had hoped that I could get at least a short furlough before I went over. To make it still harder. I could not take even your picture. I could not keep it safely, and besides regulations compelled me to send everything home. That picture would have been a sweet message to me daily. You must send me some kodaks of your own sweet self. I can carry them in my pocket.

I would like to write more, but I must close for this time.

Write me often, precious, and tell me that you love me. I want to be told often.

I love you with all my heart and soul, my darling. I know it now more than ever. I am going to be strong, Christian, and work harder because you are in my life, my life and my love.

All my love and myself are yours.

Your own,

Eugene,

Note change in address:

Co.B. 315 Sup. Train.
American Expeditionary Force,
New York City

Letter 9: June 19, 1918

My dearest Myrtle,

It seems as if a month, or, indeed, several of them, has passed since I left Camp Travis. We have been moving so much that we have scarcely had time to gather our wits.

We had a right pleasant trip. I suppose I had just as well tell you about it. Some of my narrative may prove interesting and undoubtedly some of it will bore you.

It was quite a lengthy trip, in distance traversed as well as time required for the trip. We left Camp Travis Wednesday morning at ten-forty and arrived here Monday afternoon at eight. It was not such a tiresome trip though, partly because we were passing through new country all the time. I had seen as far as Missouri before, but from there on it was all new to me. We were traveling in Pullmans too, and that of course makes it easy. A lot of these "jakes"[?] had never seen inside of a sleeper, much less traveled in one. And, as usual with a crowd of greenhorns, some ludicrous blunders were pulled. We would have been about dead on our feet if we had ridden all that distance in the chair car.

The most interesting, from a scenic viewpoint, part of the trip was here in New York State. It is hilly and in places almost mountainous. The only kind of farming that we saw in this state was truck-farming. Lots of that. Mrs. Arthur would delight in these snug little farm houses, barns, animals, gardens, etc. I would, too, if there were not much work attached to it, but—. It is a pretty state. We passed through the foothills of the Catskills. I would have enjoyed a nearer contact of these mountains, as they are so famous in song and story. We saw no real mountains at all, I was about to forget to say that we saw Lake Erie. It looked real inviting.

Missouri, Illinois, Indiana, and Ohio, were very much alike in the nature of the soil and in the general appearance of the country. Illinois and Missouri both reminded me of some parts of Texas. The prettiest bit of scenery of the whole trip was the Wabash River in Indiana and especially the town of Wabash. Wabash is the most beautiful town I ever saw. The residences are not crowded together, but have large lawns covered with closely mowed grasses. There was a profusion of larger shade trees. We passed through only a small corner of Pennsylvania. One thing that was distinctly noticeable was the increase in industries as we came east. The backing of western towns is largely farming but industrial pursuits become increasingly important as one comes east.

Oklahoma and Kansas were just like Texas, in appearance. Wheat and other grain crops gradually replaced cotton. I liked parts of Oklahoma fine. But so much for scenery. I'll tell you something about the people and the way they treated us.

The people in Texas were rather indifferent to us. Not that they cared less, I believe, but they did not show it. But people were more awake in Oklahoma and indeed for the remainder of the trip. At Duncan, Oklahoma, they came by and shook hands with us as long as our train was stopped and also at the end. At Kansas City, we hiked up town for exercise, and believe me, the people there made a noise. Handclapping and yelling were inspiring to us and we were prouder than ever of being soldiers.

Paris, MO. was another nice town. Some of the girls kissed the boys there. Other places did that, too, quite frequently. Elmira, N.Y. is the only other place that I recall as being worthy of special mention. We did not get there until ten-thirty Sunday night. But the Red Cross ladies were out with lots of lemonade and cookies. They also gave each one of us a flower. There was a tremendous crowd gathered there, the largest we saw. The people treated us fine all along the way. Nine out of every ten, or even more, would wave as we passed and wish us a safe return. Old men and women both were very enthusiastic and spry, despite their gray hairs and rheumatic joints.

I am getting along fine in my new company. Our commander is a fine man. He made a talk to us yesterday that won me for him at once. I am sure I shall get along all right.

Everybody in the supply train knows me already. An old surly looking [man] from another company heard about me and looked me up last Sunday morning. He said we wanted to have some service of some kind. I told him I would do all I could. We had two services, and, of course, I had to talk both times. I am glad to do it. I shall accept every kind of opportunity here for Christian work.

A medical lieutenant in our train is a Presbyterian from Coleman, Texas. I like him fine.

I have no idea as to how long we shall be here, and if I did have I would not be allowed to tell. I would like to tell a few more things about the last part of our trip, but the authorities will not permit it.

. . .

I think of all of you often.

Lots and lots of love, my own Myrtle.

Yours ever,

Eugene

Wednesday June 19th
Address: Eugene W. McLaurin
Co.B. 315 Sup. Train
A.E.F

Letter 10: Friday, June 25, 1918

My own Myrtle,

The greatest pleasure that has come to me since leaving Camp Travis came yesterday with the arrival of your letter.

. . .

If you could see the difficulties under which I am writing, you could doubtless pardon its scratching character. I am using the bottom of my mess kit as a writing board, and it happens to be entirely too small. However, it's the best I can do.

I know you will be delighted when you hear that I was on k.p. again yesterday. You seem to have the impression that k.p. has a purifying, or strengthening effect on my soul. I am not so sure about it. It is not so terribly hard. A fellow gets all to eat that he wants, — and that is no small want in the army. I am sure I ate a dozen oranges. This kitchen work is not entirely useless, though, for I am learning a lot of things that would be useful in a camping trip, for example to the bay. I am counting on taking such a trip some day. Nothing I have learned so far would be of much value in a kitchen. You can try me out some day and find out.

It is not at all improbable that I shall see John after I get across. In fact it is extremely probable that I shall see him often. I am pretty certain that I shall see all the home boys often. You see, the trains are a part of every army organization. There are supply ammunition and sanitary trains. The men in these various trains look after the wants of the fighting arms of the service. The ammunition train is charged with seeing that there is always plenty of ammunition, the sanitary train looks after the medical end and the supply train sees to it that the men always have food etc. You can see that there is plenty of work for each train. For example, in the supply train there are six companies of seventy-seven men each. These six companies have to distribute all food supplies to the whole division. It won't be any holiday at all, I can assure you.

. . .

You are learning more about Prussian militarism every day, I see. It hate it more and more. I knew of the manner in which the military class, especially the officers, conducted themselves towards the civilian population. It is horrible and shameless. I never cared to talk about it. It is entirely repugnant to me. Prussianism should be stamped out completely before peace comes. I, for one, don't want any peace, badly as I want peace, until it has been stamped out so it can never again menace the world's safety. I sometimes think that the Teutonic character has not changed in the least in the last twenty centuries. The difference is only on the outside. Because the extremely thin veneer of civilization, war[?] death in battle and drinking in Valhalla out of the skulls of their enemies are still abiding characteristics. I hate these things more and more every day that passes. And I have an intense hatred for everyone that supports such ideas or institutions.

Are you surprised that I express myself so violently against the Germans? I'll tell you why. My moral code is becoming exceedingly simple. It is this: whatever develops, or assists in developing, life in all its forms, as physical, mental, moral, spiritual, and special, is right and mandatory; and whatever hinders such expansion of life, or kills it entirely, is wrong and forbidden. Do you agree with me? I believe I am right. This war has brought me to this conclusion. It has destroyed so much life. When I get out, I am going to do my best to live up to it. I want to go to school and study sociology. Would you like to go? It will be hardly possible to go for two or three years after the war is over and it may never be possible, but I shall be disappointed if I don't get to go. I have a premonition that I shall go, though, I wish I could have talked over some of these things with you before I had to leave. Paisley and I often talked last winter of going to school for special work. It is sadly needed in my equipment.

Your speaking of the new records makes me long to be with you. I wish I could hear them all. I have never heard "God Be With Our Boys Tonight." It is a wonder that some of the boys here haven't bought it. They got all the new songs. We have a string band in our company that makes pretty good music. It is composed of a violin, a mandolin, and a guitar. The mandolinist (??) is a fine player. He can knock all kinds of music out of it. The music makes us all as homesick as we can be, but we would not miss it for anything in the world. You don't know how much I miss you when music starts. I don't know how much I would give to hear you playing again.

Darling, I have been thinking of you almost continually these last few days when I have time for thoughts. Most of the time my mind runs to the future, and especially, to the time when I shall return to Edna. I can't realize the joy that I shall feel then. I must not write so much about that future meeting. I get to longing for it so much that I have a queer feeling in my throat and chest. If joy can cause tears, I think they will come then.

I frequently have opportunities to do Christian work. Last night a bunch of men in a tent wanted me to lead a prayer meeting for them. It helped me lots. I hope when I get across that I shall have lots of opportunities for work in a public way. I won't get out of practice then in speaking in public. Besides it is my work and I want to work.

We fall out in ten minutes so I must close.

Remember that I love you with all my soul and life, precious darling. I am living for the day when I shall see you again. Always all my love is yours, and I am too.

Your own,

Eugene

Friday June 28, 1918

Send me some kodaks of yourself. I am anxious for them.

Bye, bye,

Eugene

Letter 11: June 1918

My own dearest Myrtle,

While all the other boys are out and everything is quiet, I am going to do a little writing. My tent mates have all got passes and gone sightseeing. I had no desire, however, to go out for only a few hours, so I am watching our tent. Someone has to stay in it, as all our equipment is here, and sometimes an article is missed.

This is some weather we are having here now. I thought I would freeze last night in spite of all that I could do. I waked up about four o'clock this morning and I was so cold that I couldn't go back to sleep until I had put on most of my clothes. What do you think of such cold weather in the month of June? It beats me. I don't know what I shall do when winter comes sure enough. I suppose I'll freeze sure enough then.

We are wearing woolen uniforms now, and I also have on a heavy Red Cross sweater. At dinner I also wore a mackinaw, that has recently been issued to us. I am glad to say that now the cold seems to be moderating somewhat. Texas is not the only state that has freakish weather.

We have been issued all of our overseas equipment now, I think. They give us something almost every hour. It is going to be quite a task to keep it all together. I was fortunate enough to get an unusually heavy Red Cross sweater. If this unseasonable weather continues, it will be worn out before winter arrives though. A little later on, I shall ask you to send me all that knitted stuff in my trunk. I can use every stitch of it, and then some, I expect. The government has issued us a muffler and a pair of leather wool-lined mittens. So you see we are not going to have any picnic next winter.

. . .

I was just wondering this morning what would be our situation now, if we had not come to an understanding when we were upstairs those all too few minutes. I can say that at least I would be worrying constantly about your attitude toward me. But now everything is settled between us until we are allowed to carry out still more of our plans. I look forward to that day with the greatest pleasure and anticipation. The reality will far surpass any imagined joy though.

. . .

I wish I could see and talk with you this afternoon. You are down at Mrs. Couchman's, of course. We could talk over all these things I am writing, if they are interesting enough, and a whole host of other things that we have not been able to talk over. We are missing the pleasure of planning together our future. Ideas have been running through my head, as they have yours too, and I am sure some of them will some day be realized. I shall be a happy man when the main event takes place. I wonder when that will be? Even a guess would be extremely uncertain.

What will the censor say if he reads this letter? He has a heart, though, and he doubtless reads so many that it becomes entirely impersonal to him. Here's hoping so at any rate.

. . .

Would you consider me inquisitive if I were to ask whether your salary was raised for next year? It should have been, even if it was not. I have been hoping you or Mrs. Arthur one would say something about it, but you didn't. This is only a 'timid suggestion' on my part.

. . .

I don't have time to worry or have the 'blues' either these days, for which I am devoutly thankful. There are enough in my tent besides myself who do worry that I can't afford it. One boy, from New Orleans, is always homesick and has the "Louisiana blues," he calls them.

This must be brought to an end, or even your patience will be exhausted. The dust gets everything dirty and writing paper is no exception. My penmanship is execrable too.

I love you with all my heart and soul, my life and my love.

Write, for I may be here some time.

Always yours,

Eugene

Sunday Afternoon

Letter 12: July 23, 1918

My own dearest Myrtle,

This is the happiest day I have known since I left Camp Travis. The explanation is that I have at last caught up with my mail. You can't know how much a letter is appreciated over here. I would not take a month's pay for today's mail, as hard up as I am. You see we have not made pay day in two months. I was gladdened with eleven letters this morning. Maybe you think I did not have two hours of the greatest pleasure in reading them. I think more of those who wrote than I ever did before. (I very absentmindedly dipped my pen into an ink bottle here and this variation is the result.) One was from Alleene and it was far and away the best letter she ever wrote me. It is of such a mature character that I can hardly realize it comes from my sister. I am prouder than ever of her. I am anxious for you and her to know each other, especially anxious for her to know you, because you are to be—well, you can finish out the sentence.

Also a letter from Mamma and one from Nina. Mamma is just the same mother, only more so. She doesn't hint at all of worry or fear for any of her boys although I know she worries more now than ever. She is brave, considering the circumstances.

. . .

We are in a quite different part of France now from what we were in when I last wrote you. And I can readily believe it is one of the most beautiful parts. It is steep and hilly at times, with pretty valleys nestling in between the hills. Wheat and other grain crops are just being harvested. The alternate green of the trees and meadows with the yellow makes an attractive scene of a little valley. I might say, in passing, that the wheat crop in France is simply fine this year. Last year it was almost a failure I have been told. France ought easily to feed herself this year, speaking out of my dense ignorance. They have truck patches everywhere. Could you guess where we are billeted? We are in a barn and it is not half bad. We have lots of wheat straw to sleep on. I had not slept on anything softer than two blankets on a wood floor in several weeks until last night. A hard floor does not bother me at all now, I am glad to say. Still one does not seek a hard floor. The barn is twice as large as the McDowell Hotel, at least in ground space, and much more substantially built if that could be possible. That is the way with all their buildings. They will stand centuries, I don't doubt. This town it is said, has one of the oldest buildings in France, an old Church. But I am afraid I don't like such buildings. The people become too much like them. They are old-timey in certain ways.

This is Sunday afternoon. It is no difficult task for me to call certain familiar scenes of Edna up before my mind. But I won't mention them here. You may know though that there is not a Sunday that passes by without my thinking of where all of you are on Sunday afternoon. How I do miss those afternoons! Some of my most pleasant memories are connected with those same afternoons.

Our top sergeant came to me just before noon and asked me if I would lead a service for the company this afternoon. Of course, I assented. It does me more good than it could possibly do any of the 'victims.' I don't want to get out of doing my chosen work. Someday I shall take it up again.

No I have not heard the sound of the guns yet. I shall have though by the time you read this, I expect. I don't know with how much trepidation I shall approach the front my first time. I rather expect I shall be a little nervous.

You ask me about my work. I don't know how much I shall be allowed to tell. In fact I don't know much about it. I am to be helper on a truck. Each truck has a corporal and a helper. Both have to know how to drive. I don't know, but I don't anticipate any trouble in learning. We carry provisions to the organizations of the divisions. At least, so far as I can gather, that is what we are to do. I don't know how near the front we shall go. Some say to within eight or ten miles of the front. Others say right up to the front. I don't know, though I am hoping to find out soon.

. . .

Are you still uncertain as to whether you have the qualifications of a minister's wife? You have had time to think about it now. I have always known, since I really know you. I have no fears at all. Like you, I am looking to the time when the day will begin and end with you. And I hope it is not so terribly far distant.

Please write more about yourself, dearest. You are more interesting to me than any Edna news. So talk about yourself more. I would not object(?) to all of it being about you.

. . .

I would like to write you more, but I am afraid this will tire out the censor.

I think I'll get all your letters now. So write as often as you can.

All my love is yours, my own Myrtle.

Yours,

Eugene

Co.B. 315 Supply Train
American Exp Forces
Via New York
CENSORED Ray Wingren[?]

Letter 13: August 14, 1918

I shall write as often as I can. If we stay here, I shall write fairly frequently. Otherwise, je ne sais pas, as the French say, "don't know." Hope I hear from you again soon.

Miss Myrtle Arthur,

Edna, Texas,
U.S.A.

My own dearest Myrtle,

I have not had an opportunity to write in the last ten days. I don't know how much time I shall have now, but I am going to begin. We may leave at any moment though, and then the chances are that what I may be able to write will be lost in a few days or so badly soiled and mutilated that I won't mail it. It is only in little snatches of time that I can write any at all.

We are busy now. The whole expedition force must be busy from what can be heard. I'll show you how my time has been spent this week and you can get some idea of what is being done over here. We have breakfast every morning at the refreshing hour of five-thirty. Really if one is awake when he eats, the early hour is bracing and invigorating. We are all up but not all are fully awake. How would that suit your royal highness? Then we go to work, work until dinner, and return as soon as we finish eating. After supper, we sometimes work, sometimes have gas drill, and sometimes get to rest. We worked all day Sunday, and had gas drill Sunday after supper. We worked all day Monday and even after supper. We worked yesterday until five o'clock when orders came to turn out on the double quick with full packs. We were tired, but we 'double timed' just the same. Then we piled into trucks and went to _____, which we reached at four o'clock this morning. About three hours of sleep, a hasty shave, (the first in several days) a run for breakfast, and we were off for our trucks.

I wrote above yesterday afternoon. We made the return trips with our trucks last night and are at "home" again. We are lined up now to be paid. As we may have to wait some little bit, I am going to do a little letter writing.

That long-delayed letter you sent me addressed to the medical detachment has at last arrived. It came Tuesday afternoon. I am almost sure that I have received all the letters you have written me since I left Camp Travis. I am glad that none of them have gone astray. Letters, especially yours, are too precious over here to lose even one. So you may be assured that all your letters will reach me. I wish I was as certain that mine would reach you. I suppose you will hear from me occasionally though. I can't find much time for writing, we are so busy. Almost the only way I can do is as I am doing now.

. . .

The statements you made in one of your recent letters (if the latter part of June may be called recent??) about the large place of prayer in your life has surprised me very much. I must confess you have been "camouflaging" if you will pardon the newness of the word in speaking of such an important feature of life, your real feelings and habits. That attitude, assumed of course, and your general character constituted a paradox for me which I could not solve. I felt that it was not your real self. In fact I knew it wasn't, that you were masquerading. But I could not prove it.

It gives me a greater feeling of safety and security to know that you are praying for me every day. I have all kinds of faith in the power of prayer, and for anyone, the more abundantly God will be with that one. That is one reason why I feel so safe. Also, you can know that we over here need prayer now more than ever. We don't have much time for prayer, unless work is prayer, which can easily be, and consequently we need help more than ever.

What do you think of the war by now? Everything is going fine. Mrs. Arthur is much nearer correct about the coming of peace than you are. All the soldiers think it will come by Christmas. And if it should hold on until spring, winter will put a stop to all fighting. The American soldiers all say on the front, "Hell, heaven or Hoboken by Christmas." It is certainly time that our forces over here are doing lots of work. No one can tell when it will end, but even the Prussians ought to be able to see that a more remote peace can only be more and more unfavorable to Germany.

This is certainly the queerest letter I have ever written. I am replacing a sheet which was "contracted" to the censor, I was afraid. That accounts for the change in paper and any abruptness. I had already finished the letter and asked our lieutenant about a little incident that I was writing you. He said it would be safer to leave it out and I have done so. But you will get a letter two pages longer as I was out of the other paper.

Since I wrote the first part of this letter, we have made a considerable "trek" over France. We have at last arrived at that much-talked-of place, the front. We are stationed several miles behind the front, quite out of reach of their guns. Some of our trucks, or maybe all of them, make a trip to the trenches every day or at night, carrying food supplies usually. This sector is rather quiet and has been so virtually since the beginning of the war. John's regiment is up there, I think but I have not been able to see him yet. I saw Milton Crawford the other day. He passed through where we were billeted before we came here. He was getting along fine. He gets to see the other Edna boys quite frequently.

I suppose you would be interested in the sensations one experience as he approaches the front. I have not run up to the front as yet, but I can hear the firing of the big guns and can see the berating of the shells at time. We have had a little excitement once or twice, but I have felt no trembling as yet. However, I fully expect them to seize me fast when I really get to the front.

We were in a barn before we moved over to this place. It was imagination, as subsequent events have proven, but I could feel all the time I was there innumerable creatures crawling over my body. It was the most disagreeable sensation I have ever experienced. It was with inexpressible relief that I discovered it was only my imagination. I am deathly afraid that I'll catch some of the parasites. None of us has been so unfortunate so far as to get them. We have fine quarters now, the best in France, we are told. All of us would be easily content to stay here for the duration of the war.

. . .

Don't worry about me, because really I am in very little danger. This is a quiet sector of the front, unusually so, and has been so for a long time.

I dreamed of all of you a few nights ago. You can imagine how disappointed I was when I found it was only a dream. It is a rare thing for me to dream, and this one was so vivid.

Tomorrow is Sunday. I hope to be able to attend a service of some kind. That is a rare privilege now. A whole heart full of love for you.

Yours,

Eugene

E.W. McLaurin
Co.B 315 Sup. Train
American Ex. France
Roy Wingren[?]

Letter 14: August 30, 1918

My own dearest Myrtle,

I am sitting flat down on a sidewalk as I make this epistolary effort. You need not be surprised at such a seat, as chairs are a rare luxury over here. I haven't sat in a chair in ages. How long is it going to take the Americans who stayed at home to re-civilize this bunch of soldiers? I often wonder whether we can be again as we once were. I am extremely anxious to find out whether I have forgotten the proper use of a bed. It will be with a sign of happy contentment that I fall into a bed at home or at Edna. A real bed again,—well, it is almost beyond the reach of imagination at present.

Another thing that I want to experience is the pleasure of sleeping late in the morning, say until seven o'clock. Have you ever heard Harry Lander's record, "It's nice to get up in the Morning, but it's nicer still to lie in bed"? I am going to buy it when I get to America and get someone to play it on the Victrola. We get up at five o'clock every morning. It is a rather difficult thing to do. One rarely achieves it without the gentle aid of a sergeant.

We had a dandy breakfast this morning, eggs, beef, biscuit, gravy, butter, syrup and coffee. Of course we did not get these in wholesale lots, especially the eggs, biscuit, and butter. But there was enough to satisfy a reasonable appetite. Eggs are some higher than in America. In San Antonio last winter they were seventy cents a dozen as well as I remember. They are about ninety cents over here. This was a real American meal. Don't think though that it is the customary thing. It is quite the contrary. But we always have nourishing food and nearly always at regular hours. Sometimes work must be done at once. If it does not require too long, we finish the work before eating.

We have been in this camp now a week. All of us are quite contented to remain here an indefinite period—unless, of course, the Germans retreat so far that we can not do our work from here. It would be a fine place to hibernate, if we have to spend the winter in France. We have good sleeping quarters, good baths, and are near a good-sized town. However, it will be only by rare good fortune that we shall stay here so long as that. I visited this town yesterday for the first time. As you can easily imagine, it has many sights and scenes interesting to an American. All the streets are narrow. Some of the streets are so narrow that carriages cannot pass each other in them. The sidewalks also are narrow. Some of them are so narrow, and at the same time sloping outward, that one person walks them with difficulty. These towns are built hundreds of years ago, most of them and their builders could not foresee the need for wider streets, etc. I am anxious to go to this town again. I want to see more of it. There is an old cathedral there that I am especially anxious to see. I have not seen the inside of a church of any description since I came to France. It is interesting also to observe the shoppers every morning, the women especially. They carry bags for their purchases of vegetable, dry goods etc. No delivery wagons here.

[End of this letter missing]

Letter 15: September 3, 1918

Somewhere Else In France.

Another war to our credit. It seems that we never stay more than a few days at one place. We did not move so very far though this time. We are in the woods now and have a right nice camping place. Of all things! Since I began this page, orders have come to load all our stuff on trucks. Another move of course. One nice thing about it though is that it is very little trouble to move. This letter will have to be continued once more. Don't you get tired of seeing so many new beginnings in every letter? It seems that I can never finish a letter at one sitting. So long until I have another opportunity.

What do you think of the war news these days? The Boches seem to be retreating whenever they are attacked strongly. The British have been doing some fine work during the last two weeks. The French have not been idle either. I'll be glad when the Americans get into the fight in strength. It will cost us heavily, I suspect, as victory must always cost.

. . .

I have made a resolution during the last few days, but I'll wait and tell you face to face. I can't begin to carry it out until I am with you again anyway.

A whole heart full of love for you.

Your own,

Eugene

E.W. McLaurin
Co.B. 315th Sup. Train
American Exped. Force
Ray Wingren
Lt. I. M.P.N.D.[?]

Letter 17: September 26, 1918

Dearest Myrtle,

It has been quite a while since I have had time to write you. You can easily understand this long silence when you know what has been happening during the last few weeks. I don't know how much I shall be able to write you now, as we may receive order at any time to move.

My work has changed its nature considerably since I last wrote you. At that time I had the nominal position of interpreter for my company commander. In reality I was doing nothing. Finally, I asked to be put on a truck, and did make one lone trip. That ended, at least so far as I can tell at present, my "position" (?) in the supply train. Two weeks and somewhat more ago, I was assigned to this regiment as acting-chaplain. Mr. Reese now directs the religious work of the ____, and his promotion left the regiment without a chaplain. Only the day before I was ordered over here, I had talked with him of applying for a chaplain. You know I have been anxious lately to get into work of a distinctive religious character. So my opportunity came sooner than I expected. Of course I am as ignorant as a child, almost, of the technical work of a chaplain. I shall learn though. I am getting out an application today for a commission as chaplain. This is too much about myself though.

Well, I have been to the front and 'over the top.' I wish I could tell you about it all, but space is too limited, and a few things might not get by the censor. I did not know what the special duties of a chaplain were when his organization went into battle. I was anxious to do something, because inaction was getting on my nerves. I volunteered as a stretcher bearer and went over just after the first wave. Most of the wounds were light and the men could usually walk. Sometimes we had to assist them, and sometimes we carried them on litters. I will tell you one incident that occurred, just to give you an idea of what was going on. I found a man who had been gassed. He was able to walk but we had to proceed slowly, as gassed patients must not exert themselves. The Boche artillery was firing on us, making lots of noise of noise [written twice] and straightening out any kinks in our hair but only occasionally wounding a man. Just as we started the artillery fire increased, and we had to stop in a shell hole. It took me about two hours to get that man and another to the first aid station. That first aid work appeals to me. The men are always so brave, and cheerful.

I want to tell you about their artillery fire. Fritz uses lots of artillery, but I don't dread it nearly so much as I thought I would. It makes lots of noise and you will think you and the whole vicinity are going on a swift joy ride. But the explosion comes, you jump up from where you have thrown yourself on the ground, and find that about the only damage done is to your nervous system. Shells pass over this village occasionally, but the soldiers regard them indifferently, unless, indeed, it seems to be coming directly towards us. Then they scamper. A shell always gives notice of its coming. Sometimes this notice is exceedingly brief, but there is plenty of time to fall to the ground and flatten out. A man doesn't look for a nice smooth spot on which to fall, but ducks into mud, rocks, bushes, or anything that may happen to be around him. And he doesn't express any regrets either. For any damage to his clothes or his person. Artillery fire, though it is not by any means harmless, is yet not so destructive of human life.

I haven't a very high opinion of Fritz as a fighter. He is not fair and sportsmanlike. When chances break even, he hikes, or else throws up his hands and yells "comrade." That is what gets me. If I were fighting, I would not take every advantage of my opponent and then, when we were on an equal footing, quit. Fritz is a bad fighter, or perhaps poor fighting is better. I don't want to convey the impression that I have no respect for him when his guns are turned on me. I have a profound respect, especially if he is at a considerable distance. And I try to seek a safe place. But, in any and every circumstance, he is not a good soldier.

What do you want for a souvenir? I have seen a lot of things that would make suitable souvenirs. Everything from machine guns and concrete pill boxes in profusion to little knick-knacks of various kinds. The Germans say the Americans are crazy for souvenirs. They leave some nice ones too. To walk into some of their dugouts, one would not think that they had left according to a prearranged plan. If they do, they certainly leave a lot of stuff. You can believe too all that you hear about loaded fountain pens, etc. I saw one poor fellow who tried to open a German canteen. As for me, I have not tried to open anything German.

Do you remember four months ago today? Of course, that is a fool-
ish question. But I have been thinking of it after today. I suppose you are
teaching school, if the schools have yet opened. I wish I could have been
in Edna on September 17. You recall that long ride last year on that date.
But all those things seem far away now. You may not hear from me very
often. I shall write as often as I can though. I can't understand why I don't
hear more often from you. I have not heard in three weeks. Maybe they
will all come at one time. I have had several letters in that time from Mrs.
Arthur. I can't understand it at all. John hears from you. I see him every
day. He is looking fine.

As Ever,

Eugene

Letter 18: October 4, 1918

My own Myrtle,

. . .

I was in a town yesterday that the Huns had to leave in haste. It was
evidently an important center. They departed in such haste that they left
everything in an indescribable confusion. Some of the officers must have
had their wives and children there.

Dresser drawers, wardrobes, etc. had been emptied of their contents
and scattered pellmell on the floor. I saw nice expensive broadcloth coats
and capes, and skirts, piled up in a heap with all other kinds of clothes. I
saw a soldier come prancing out of a building with a hightop silk hat and an
expensive claw-hammer coat on and parade around, quite a contrast to his
comrades. I saw just worlds of chinaware and some silverware. Very little
of the crockery broken, although the town had been subjected to severe
shelling by both the sides. There has been lots of jam there, but it did not
last long before the vicious onslaughts of hungry American soldiers.

I went into the church. It has been shelled pretty badly. Several shells
had scored a direct hit and one or two had exploded inside the church.
Not a window but has suffered. The altar though and every image was in
place. The French had already been there and set up a cast of Joan of Arc
in armor with a background of three French flags. They have this figure
in every church that I have been in. This church that I have been telling

you of was over three hundred years old. They are all substantially built and in addition to the ravages of old Father Time, make a noble resistance against modern German artillery.

Do you think you can endure a description of life in a modern dugout? I'll describe this one as it is my present "home."

This particular dugout was a German aidstation or hospital. It has three rooms at the entrance the walls of which are of masonry or concrete about four feet thick. From these rooms there are three entrances to the dugout itself which is about thirty-five feet underground. Sixteen of us sleep in the dugout, the officers sleep in the three rooms. We have bunks, in single uppers and lowers. I think I sleep all right. The other night I was not feeling very well and was tired out too. So I went to bed early, at seven-thirty, and got up the next morning at eight-thirty. Can you believe it? It sounds more like some of your tricks.

We have a stove, and every night we make us a good warm fire.

The other night we had some real hotcakes and sugar syrup. However, the grease and smoke almost "gassed" our officers.

The conversation is extremely broad, at times, on such topics as the present world war, the possibilities of an early peace, the internal condition of Germany, America after-the-war policy, etc. Then again each one will tell how close he has been to some of Fritz's shells. Some man will come on and ask about Fritz. Every changing mood of this notorious individual is worthy at least passing notice. The name given to his shells is "G-I-Cans." "G.I" is an abbreviation for galvanized iron. G.I. Cans are about twenty inches or two feet in diameter and about thirty or thirty-six inches high and are used for water, go waste, or around the kitchen. Some nights Fritz is lavish with his G-I-Cans. Others, he is quiet.

Sometimes a song is started, such as "Back Home Again In Indiana," or of a like quality. But it does not get very far, partly because there is no good singer here, and partly because men don't like to sing such songs. Of course, there is the usual number of stories, true and untrue. One fellow has just been entertaining the crowd with a recital of his experiences and doings at a western meeting. One of the many things this cowboys says he did was to drop his knife, point first, on a frog's back, causing quite a commotion. But I must make an end of all this. It may give you an idea of life in a dugout, though.

Say, that was rich about those two letters that got censored. I rather think that none of Mamma's ever passed the censor. It was full of things which we thought at the time we could write. Since, however, we have learned better. It was a good one on me all right. However, I am not troubled at all that my home folks saw it. I just don't care, since you say there was nothing much in it.

The future looks fine now. I am still hoping that peace will come by Christmas. God have pity on this old world. It will take a long time for peace to heal the wounds of this war.

You are in my thoughts more than ever, and I hope it won't be many months until I shall be with you again.

Lots of love.

Yours,

Eugene

Censored

Letter 19: October 20, 1918

My own dearest Myrtle,

. . .

We have moved since I last wrote you. We did not go very far though. We made the move in trucks. I am sure glad we did not have to hike. We are now on a front where one of the biggest German drives took place. You would recognize it at once if I were to call the name. Some rather hot fighting has occurred on this sector. There is no telling when we shall go up to the front. We don't know what we are going to do in fact.

How would you like a walk tonight in this drizzling rain? I am going over about two miles and get today's paper from the Y.M.C.A. for my battalion. They give us about forty of fifty papers for the whole battalion of four companies. Of course that doesn't go very far, but we are very glad indeed to get that much. We are anxiously awaiting developments these days, and a newspaper is always eagerly read. I get the papers back to our quarters and scatter out to the companies by about eight-thirty or nine o'clock. You can't know how glad they are to get the papers. Then I come back to my shack where the battalion runners and I stay. Then I make myself comfortable and digest the contents of the paper.

. . .

Yes, the division was in action at the time you speak of and we had a hand in bagging those prisoners. None of the Edna boys was injured at all. Of course we can tell some bloody-curdling stories, but you will have to allow for the stress of undue excitement and also the innate human tendency to exaggerate.

I hope you all are getting a lot of my letters. I suppose you are missing some of them at any rate. I have been writing all along. I am not getting half of your letters. Don't know what happens to the others. But that is all right. I would much rather that you all should get my letters than that I should get yours. Isn't that conceit? I know that you and the others worry about us, and for that reason I hope my letters all go through safely.

Remember that I love you with all my heart and am waiting for that day when we shall see each other again.

With all my love,

Eugene

Letter 20: November 13, 1918

My own dearest Myrtle,

Ain't it a grand and glorious feeling? This may not be grammatically correct, but it is certainly expressive at this time. I have not yet been quite able to adjust myself to the new style of living which has burst upon us. So many of the conveniences of life as it used to be are now missing. (My pen is so bad I must fall back on a pencil. Fountain pens get extremely dry at the front. Please pardon the pencil this time though.) For example, it was almost an unheard of thing to think of passing a night without the disturbing boom of guns or more dreadful still, the screech and crash of shrapnel. But now the long night through one never hears a cannon or a shell. And again you don't have to keep your eyes on every visible airplane and be ready to duck or "flatten out," if he cuts off his engine and starts toward you with his machine gun sputtering away like mad. And best of all you don't wonder and dread the order to go up to the front and go over the top. Any man might want to go the first time. Only a blank idiot or a fool would wish for the second time over the top. Of course, we would go, if it were necessary. But we are all very, very thankful that it is not necessary. Yes, it is a rather grand and glorious feeling.

While I am rambling along "chasing rabbits" as Dr. Sampson used to say when he followed stray thoughts or suggestions that came to his mind, I'll tell you of what a close call our regiment has. That is, how near it came to going over the top of the morning that the armistice went into effect. You know that the papers say the armistice was signed up at five-forty A.M. Monday Nov. 11. Well, my battalion and one other from our regiment were scheduled to go over the top at six A.M. the order to keep their present positions came in time to check the advance. They were a happy bunch of men, believe me. It was (about) about a hundred yards to the Germans and they had all kinds of machine guns. Our boys would have taken them but it would have cost, and the loss of a single life would have been useless, because the war was won.

Do you think that I have entirely forgotten you? It certainly seems so, for I have not written you in three weeks. (It seems like as many months.) But we have been busy during those weeks. We were heavily underscoring "Armistice" for Fritz. And it was well, don't you think? Our regiment gave him a good start at the opening of the drive on our narrow front and our and other regiments kept pressing him. It was more of a victory though than I dreamed of at the time.

Here I have gone astray again. I was trying to find some excuse for not having written you. But so many things have been impressed, indelibly on my mind during these last few weeks that it is easy to follow some 'rabbit' that crosses my path. If I had had the time, I could have written you, if I had had paper. But we were taking only the necessities of life then. Two blankets, a rain coat, and reserve rations of hard tack and corned beef—"Corn Woolley," the boys call it. I wish I had the time to tell you some of the things I have seen. But your patience would give out. I am thankful that I am in the condition I am at present. I have come through without a scratch. To be sure, I have not been exposed much. Still I am thankful that God has kept me. I have never thought since coming over here that Fritz would get me, not because I was luckier or anything like that, but because so many good people were praying for me. I believe that just as firmly as I believe anything. Prayer was certainly answered. But keep on praying for me just as normal.

I am already planning what I shall do when I get back to the States. Of course that may be a long time off yet. Still, it does not hurt to dream and plan. I feel sure that I shall be in Edna long before school closes. Ergo, I shall have the pleasure of taking you to and from school once more. And other and bigger things come into my mind too. I can hardly imagine what the first day with you will be like. I know I shall be happy. And then there will be many more such days, and better ones, too, perhaps to follow.

. . .

I am feeling somewhat lonely and blue tonight. It is unusual for me to be in such a frame of mind. I have not had time to think lately and now that I do have a little time and especially since hostilities have ceased and we are turning lingering looks towards the dear old States, it somehow works on my feelings. I suppose it will soon pass away.

I am sorry that I have written the above. It will only cause you to worry. It is nothing. But I certainly do long to see you and the others, you and my mother especially. I had letters from each of you today, and both of them were unusually good too. Maybe I shall get more mail now. I am glad that you are hearing from me at least occasionally. I have tried to write once a week on an average, since I came to France. I shall be glad when I can censor my own mail. It will at least get off then, whether it reaches you or not.

. . .

You remark on my optimism about the war. I cannot refrain from mentioning this, since fighting was over before I got your letter in which you told me the fighting would not be over until next summer. I am glad you do not always tell the truth though. It would mean lots of work over here. But I shall see you long before summer arrives again.

We are in a part of France that is not so badly marked by the ravages and destruction of war as some of the country behind us. They did not have time to take positions and hold them. The fields are only occasionally marked by shell holes. There is a town seven kilometers northeast of this little place where civilians have been during all the war. They were under German rule all that time. They were happy people when the Americans played in the square there and closed with the "Marseillaise" and "The Star Spangled Banner." When they heard their national air,— it was the first time in four years. The tears just coursed down their cheeks. The Germans were severe on them, as usual. Fines for so-called offenses were common.

I rode back in a Red Cross Ambulance from that town. The only patient was a French boy of about ten years old who had been wounded in one arm and one leg by shrapnel. He was being taken back to an

American hospital. I asked him several times if he was suffering. He always said "no." He was a brave little chap. Several of them were wounded.

Like even a long sermon, a long letter must finally end. This is the longest letter I have written in some time. Do you feel flattered?

Lots and lots of love, my own Myrtle— All my love is yours.

As ever,

Eugene

Letter 21: November 17, 1918

My own dearest Myrtle,

I have several things that I could be doing tonight, but I really desire to do only one thing. This is Sunday night you know, and Sunday night always recalls pleasant memories, as also does Sunday morning. This has seemed more like Sunday than any other Sunday I have spent in a long, long time. We had a memorial service this morning in respect to the men who have made the supreme sacrifice and gift in our cause. This afternoon I stayed in my rooms (do well to have part of one room) and wrote. We had all the regiments together for the service this morning. All except the first battalion. It has moved several miles forward, or parallel. I certainly hated to see them leave and me stay behind, but I could not do otherwise without having a lot of work on Chaplain Lewis' hands. But I am in hopes that I shall soon follow.

I think we can catch up with our work in one more day. If we do, and stay here a day or two longer, I want to do some sightseeing. The scenery here is beautiful. Several high hills extend out into the valley like fingers. I have never been on one of the high hills and am anxious to observe the landscape from such a vantage point. Visibility is usually fine, for it seems that with the cessation of firing, the sun is beginning to smile on this country. If the sun is not shining, it is always hazy and foggy, and perhaps raining.

There is a little church upon a hill break of this town that I am anxious to visit. It is apparently a real nice building and has only two shell holes in it. There is also another church about a quarter of a mile from here that is very interesting. I have not visited it as yet either.

I took a little vacation last Friday and visited my old company in the supply train. It was the first time I had been back to them since I was detached and assigned to my present duties. I would see one of the boys occasionally but not to talk to them very long at the time. They were all safe and sound. One sergeant had been hit by a piece of shrapnel in his forehead, and it barely broke the skin, the boys said. But it was almost ridiculously amusing how conspicuous he contrived to make his wound stripe. The boys laugh at him a lot. I have seen a lot of boys who were really wounded, who would not wear them. I am thankful to say that I have come through without a single scratch. Well, I did cut my finger pretty deeply once, but that was with a safety razor. As a matter of fact, I never had any idea of receiving a wound. I sometimes had doubts as to how I would get out at times, but I pulled through fine.

. . .

It makes me downright mad for all of you all to be mentioning pies, cakes, fried chicken, etc. all the time. You have committed the crime several times. Nina is a habitual offender. Did you all make any potatoes this year? Sweet potatoes I mean? Nina was teasing my appetite in her last letter by mentioning potatoes. If you don't remember just ask Mrs. Arthur whether I like fried sweet potatoes or not. I would give twenty-five francs for all of them and real biscuit and butter that I could eat at one time. I have given orders home to reserve some potatoes for me, to be eaten next February. I am going to do some eating when I get back.

. . .

Remember always that you are ever in my thoughts and your image is enshrined in my heart. I can think oftentimes when I can't do anything else. And my thoughts always turn to you. Sometimes I wonder what you are doing just at the particular time. Or I wonder what you would say and think if you could see me sometimes, in various and sundry plights. Most of all though, I wonder what we would be doing if I were with you and the others. Not with them all all the time, of course, but sometimes with just you alone. These are the sweetest and most encouraging thoughts that come to me, and you may be sure that I linger and ponder over them. You are inexpressibly dear to me, Myrtle, and the dearest plans that I have in my life are those in which you take the largest part. I shall certainly be pleased when we can talk over these plans together, don't forget that you mean more and more to me every day the fact that your love and you yourself in all the strength and goodness of your character are mine, in prospect at least, is the most cheering and inspiring element in my life, in a human way you understand. I try to live as Christ would want me to live, but He expects us to help and to be helped by, and very much too, our friends and acquaintances. But I am saying too much. You will think I am flattering you. But it is sincere, every word of it.

. . .

I have written more on these intimate personal thoughts of mine in this letter tonight that I have in a long time before. But it is because I am somewhat lonely tonight after so many weeks of hard work and strain. This being away from you, the Edna people, and my home folks goes against my grain. I like to be around a home. A man in the army never sees anything like that.

. . .

Does Howe regret not getting into service? If he is very much of an idiot, he does. If he is sensible, he won't. That is, at his age. I am thankful that only three of us were in it. If Mamma knew— but I'll pass that up. You have said something in several letters about that resolution that I have made and you want [me] to tell you. It is scarcely worthy of so much space. Still I can hardly tell you until I see you. I would much rather tell you face to face than to write it. You would prefer it that way too, if you only knew. However, I am carrying out the resolution in every letter to you, just as I expect to carry it out every day when I am with you. So please wait. I am living it as well as I can now. Distance makes it almost impossible though.

All my love is yours, my own Myrtle.

Yours,

Eugene

Letter 22: November 25, 1918

My dearest Myrtle,

. . .

This battalion was the first allied soldiers to enter this (kitchen I am crazy; a boy mentioned kitchen and that is the mecca of a soldier's longings these days) town. They came in Sunday, November 17, at noon. The Germans had barely left the town. Some of the inhabitants were in cellars. All were inside. They say they were afraid it was another "Boche trick." You can more easily imagine the welcome they gave our men and the gladness at being once more free of German government, or rather Prussian militarism. Their joy knew no bounds. They danced, sang, paraded, and cried. Just anything that could even partly express their strong emotion. The Belgians seem to enjoy singing the "Marseillaise," as though it belonged to them. It is the most inspiring song I have ever heard, I believe. Last night a crowd passed me on the street singing in unison and as lustily as they could. Believe me, I can easily feel why that is the most famous national air in the world.

We have fine quarters now. I think the days and nights in muddy trenches and mud holes, or "fox holes" they are called, are over. No more nights out in the rain with only a "pup" tent over you and a blanket, or perhaps two to wrap up in. The three buildings our battalion are in face a quadrangle and, before the war, were a school of about grammar school and high school grades combined. It is called the "Gymnasium." The Germans left it in a filthy condition. And it was filth that was the accumulation of time and not of haste and confusion. The quadrangle was deep with hay, empty cans and other such trash. When the Belgians here saw that we were going to clean up a little bit at any rate, they willingly helped with wagons and men. They built sheds for our kitchens and also have kept us in wood.

I should have said earlier that I was not able to come up with the battalion as Chaplain Lewis and I had to pack up in small parcels and list in triplicate, the contents of each of our men who was killed. It required care and was tedious and slow. So I did not come up until Thursday.

When I first came to Virton, I thought the Belgians did not hate the Germans as much as the French do. They never say "Les Boches, pas bons," ("Boches no good"), or anything like that, until you have known and talked to them. But their hatred is much more intense than that of the French.

Today I was in a drug store when two German nurses started to come in. I had not seen them, but the clerk let us know of their presence. She fairly hissed "Les Boches!" Then she spoke as the Germans came in and said "Bon jour, mademoiselles!" They have been trained to conceal their hatred, but it is strong and will remain there for many a day. A queer thing is that the Belgians refer to the Germans as "Les Boches," but always it is "Les Allemandes." That also is due to the continued presence of the Germans among them.

I mention the German nurses just now. We got in behind the Germans and were pushing them so hard that they did not have time to remove their wounded. Four hundred are in a hospital here. The Germans left a full medical staff and supplies and equipment, except food. There were four Americans in the hospital. These have since been evacuated to an American hospital. They received the best of treatment from the Germans, they said. They were fed five times a day, just as the Germans were. One man had lost an arm and a leg and was pulling along fine. That is a serious operation, you know.

The Germans tried to make the Belgians here work for them. It was work, or suffer. And in every case that I have heard of, they refused to turn a hand. The result was that they suffered. No one was killed here in this town, but I have talked to lots of men who were beaten or starved. But they actually killed even women and children in a little village near here.

Civil prisoners and refugees and prisoners of war are coming through here all the time. All of them report a great scarcity of food in Germany. Coffee, of a good grade, is worth about seven dollars and a half here. The Germans use the leaves of trees for coffee, prisoners say. They say that the Germans simply could not feed them. On an average they got as much almost as the German soldier. But for the life of me, I cannot understand how the Germans fought so long on such a small amount of food. I would have "revolted" or yelled "camarade" long ago. Some of the prisoners are thin and emaciated beyond belief almost. An English lad, of about eighteen apparently, placed my hand on his thigh. It wasn't a bit larger than my arm. He had just wasted away. It may be, though, that the Germans discriminated against the British. They hate England bitterly and England returns it with good interest.

I am sending you some interesting reading. It is a great (?) American paper that I have run across. It is a small phase of the field covered by German propogandism. I read today a paper published for the French inhabitants of occupied territories. It is exceedingly light reading. And its logic is without a flaw! Keep it as a souvenir of German literature.

. . .

You have already learned from the papers of the part our division is to play in the army of the occupation. Only two national army divisions are in this army. The nineteenth, quite naturally and as might be expected, is one of them. I don't know what we are to do, but I suppose we shall soon be in

Germany. I am in hopes a responsible government will be quickly formed at Berlin and allow us to go home. But we shall see some new country.

It is certainly a pleasure and a relief to get out of wartorn territory. Everywhere one would see shell holes, shattered trees, and wrecked houses. On every side only destruction was evident. We came through part of the old Verdun battlefield. It was, absolutely, the most desolate area I have ever seen. As we came on further, the desolation diminished, but everywhere and always there was some visible, silent reminder of war. But after we passed our front line positions on the day that the armistice was signed the reminder of war steadily diminished until soon there was not the least evidence of fighting. It seems as though we have been transported into another world into a natural, real, sensible world. War is a terrible strange nightmare. One feels that it is unnatural, unreal, and senseless. A man's soul and body are both in a stress and strain. Oftentimes I have wondered if I would not awake suddenly and find the whole thing a dream. Thank God, it is an experience at least, and not a present reality. It is all past and gone. And may a merciful God keep the world from such a calamity in the future. Thanksgiving comes this week. Won't it be a real Thanksgiving! We are all thankful, and your birthday comes this week. Many many happy returns of that day. (Don't think I deliberately and maliciously placed Thanksgiving and your added year in the same paragraph. It was accidental.)

Best wishes for a pleasant Thanksgiving and a joyous Christmas.

With my love,

Eugene

Letter 23: December 18, 1918

My dearest Myrtle,

I am going to try to write you tonight, but it may be a poor effort. If you could witness what happens in this room, you would readily agree with me. One boy is playing a French harp. Of course every piece he plays makes me think of home. It would be hard to play anything that did not make us think of that place. This is a homesick bunch tonight anyway. One fellow from Louisiana is so homesick that it sticks out all over him. He has been that way for several days. A boy named Glenn from east Texas also plays. He is redheaded and chews lots of tobacco, but in spite of these faults, he is a pretty good fellow. He is a runner and is the only runner remaining of those who came up to the front as runners. Every once in a while, he breaks out, in mournful tones, such as you hear in negro songs:

"I don't care for nobody much;

Nobody cares for me."

It is terribly lonesome and depressing. I have not been very homesick as yet, because I know it is useless. None the less, I am a little anxious to get back.

He is playing "The Baggage Coach Ahead." Isn't it queer that soldiers like sad pieces? I have often noticed it. They always like "Where is My Wandering Boy Tonight?" But there is one song that I have never yet heard called for. That is "Home, Sweet Home." It is simply too sad and hits too close to home.

Well, we are in Germany and not very far from the Rhine either. Who would have thought two months ago that so soon our armies would be so far into Germany? It almost surpasses belief to think that it is actually real. This whole dream is unreal to me. I'll surely be glad when it is ended.

I'll tell you something about our hike. It may be interesting to you over there. Perhaps you can trace it on the maps.

We left Marville, France on the last day of November. Although that section of France was not the scene of any actual fighting, still it showed signs of war. Many of the towns were quite deserted. Some of the inhabitants had retreated before the invading Huns and most of the others fled a few days before the armistice on the eve of the approaching battle. You remember that the Germans were doing "To the rear, March" pretty fast, and they had notified all the nations to get fifty or seventy five miles behind the front. Most of the fields had lain idle two, or three, and perhaps even four years. It was a relief to get out of sight of such sights.

It was at Longuyon that I first saw one sign of "Kultur," of which the world has had only many reports, and true ones too. Longuyon is quite an important manufacturing center, at least it was before the war. It has foundries and rolling mills galore. All these plants have been robbed of everything portable. It is hard to believe, but all the heavy machinery, as well as the window lights, doors, etc., had been removed. Of course Germany will have to replace it. It is only justice.

At Pierre Pont, a small village near the France-Luxemburg frontier, affords another example of their practices. The Germans were practically in haste to evacuate all occupied territory and naturally did many things that perhaps they might not have done under other circumstance. In this town were about forty French and American wounded. They had been brought hastily from the front by the Germans and had not been removed even from the cars. They did not get any medical attention, food, or water, for a period of two days. The natives of the town slipped them water and food at night, but it was with difficulty. As soon as the armistice was declared, a girl from the village made her way to our lines and told them of the situation at Pierre-Port. They acted promptly and a medical unit motored into the town before the Germans left it. They ministered to the wounded at once. This incident compares very unfavorable with their treatment of our wounded in Virton, Belgium. I hope this was only an isolated instance and not a general practice.

Our line of march led us through a part of German Lorraine. At least it has been German for the last forty eight years. The Germans call it [Lotharingia], I believe, but Lorraine is a corruption of [Lotharingia], I am told. We knew at once that we had stepped into a new country. We passed through a manufacturing town whose name I do not at present recall. It was as spick and span as could be. The plants were not running, but the buildings and machinery were all polished and shining just like new. And it was all there too. The children in school have had to study and speak German. French is "verboten." The older people could speak French, but only a very few of the children could handle it at all.

On December 2, we crossed into Luxemburg at Esch. It is quite a nice town. Many of the inhabitants are French or Belgian in ancestry. The Luxembougiose were quite warm towards us. The little children caught our hands and walked down the street with us, sometimes quite a distance. They had their flags flying everywhere. Occasionally we saw a French flag in Luxemburg. In France, of course, they were abundant. In Germany, however, we have not seen a single flag. They don't show them at all.

We spent that night at Dudelange (or Dudelingen), the next at Aspelt and the next two at Kleinmacher, a little village near Remich on the Moselle. We were given a day's rest here and we were rather in need of it too.

On December 6, we made our triumphant entry into Germany. With our regimental and national colors flying, and with the band playing we crossed over the bridge over the Moselle River at Remich. The movie man was present to record it for the future, and I suppose some day you may see it. When we crossed the bridge we passed into enemy territory. It gave me a strange feeling at first, but it soon wore off. We spent that night at a little village called Beurig, on the Saar River, just opposite Saarburg. Saarburg is a nice sized town. Our next stop was near Trier, on the Moselle, I believe the English speaking world calls it Treves. It is a city. Streetcars were running there, the first I have seen in several months. We passed through Trier on Sunday. It presented quite a holiday appearance, with the inhabitants all dressed up, and no one at work. In Treves, are ruins of an old fort which goes back to Roman times. I saw also the ruins of an old castle and baths which is said to date from Constantine.

Our next stop was at Schweich, another good sized town. The people here were most cordial to the Americans. I wrote Mrs. Arthur about the former German officer and his wife, who gave us hot coffee and nice warm feather beds. Their conduct is almost unbelievable. They are certainly glad that the Americans came into this country. They say they like us much better than they do either the French or the English. Perhaps it [is] more correct for me to say that they hate us less than they do either the French of the English. Of course, it is difficult to know where sincerity stops and hypocrisy begins in their actions. It is also difficult to know how far they have been "coached" to show their goodwill, and how far it is spontaneous.

We left Schweich Monday, December 9, and stopped that night at a little village called Selansen[?]. About the only interesting thing that I remember about this place is the church. It is a large magnificent building. Inside, it is nicely finished. The main point of interest is the corner of the church given over to relics. I had often heard of such relics but it was my first time to see them. They are collected as witnesses of so-called miraculous cures effected by prayers at a certain place, or by the performance of some other specified religious duty. I saw arms, legs, crutches, etc. there. Can you believe that people in this age could credit such superstitions and impostures? It surpasses belief. Whenever I see an uplifted cross at a watering place or the forks of a road, or a shrine by the roadside, I always think of the first words of Paul in his speech on Mars Hill at (absolutely crazy!) the areopagus at Athens: "Men of Athens. I perceive that in all things ye are too superstitious." They have religious observances and festivals in abundance, but it fails to have any vitalizing effect upon the life of the people. Every home has a number of crucifixes, and I suppose every individual has also. You see them in all public places. Many of them are so aged that the elements have eroded them until the original outlines are scarcely traceable. But I have never yet seen any act of worship anywhere except in a church. The religion these people practice does not at all coincide with our ideas of religion. From our viewpoint it is as lifeless and void of power as the rock out of which these emblems are carved.

Our next stop was at Neuerberg, and the next at Bremm, about four miles down the Moselle from Alf. We rested two days in Bremm, and after six days of steady marching with heavy packs it was highly appreciated. We left Bremm on Saturday, December 14, and doubling back through Alf, stopped for the night at Hontheim. We reached Mehren the next day and this place on Monday. This rest of three days has been greatly appreciated too. We are beginning to feel fit once more. It will be a day of great joy when our hiking days are over.

It has been snowing occasionally today. It is not quite cold enough for it to stay on the ground except in certain places. It has rained every day for the last several weeks, it seems to me. It rains here just as easily as it does in south Texas. It makes it extremely disagreeable. However, we do not stir around very much. And, for a change, we are not in a barn, but a building that bears the coat-of-arms of the German Empire. It is somewhat similar to our courthouses. So we are comfortable enough. There is not much snow until January and February, the people tell us.

Can you realize that Christmas is almost upon us? I can't. Only six days and the date of the year will be here. But it won't be a real Christmas to most of us over here. Christmas boxes are beginning to come in, but at last reports Mamma hadn't received my label. Like so many of my letters it must have wondered off to unknown regions.

. . .

My love for you grows day by day and I am anxiously awaiting the time when we shall be together again.

With my love,

Eugene

Letter 24: December 26, 1918

My own dearest Myrtle,

What kind of a Christmas have you had this year? It is already over, if it passed as quickly in the States as it did over here. I suppose all of you went to Mrs. Couchman's and also took dinner there. Even though I could not be there for the celebrations, I thought of all of you and wished for you a Merry Christmas. It was a happy Christmas all over the world, even though so many of us were away from home. It was a real Christmas once more of "Peace on earth." You can hardly realize how glad we are that we are not spending this Christmas in the mud, water, and cold of the trenches. We ourselves don't realize it for we have never experienced real winter warfare. But we have seen enough to make us all dread it.

Well, at last, I think the period of wandering is over and we shall remain here until we begin the home stretch for the "Promised Land." And, believe me, everyone is glad that we are through hiking, from Major General O'Neil, our division commander, down to the K.P.'s and dog robbers. We had been fed up on it until we had enough to last us for a long, long time. In fact, I think I have entirely caught up with my walking. A lady out in West Texas once said that Texas women would ride to the kitchen to wash the dishes, if they only could. I am even worse. I am not going to walk except when I have to. We have hiked about two hundred miles altogether, I suppose.

I spent Christmas as I did last Christmas, hard at work. The Y.M.C.A. had a lot of stuff to give to my battalion, but it had not been sorted out and put in the little Christmas packages. I promised the Y.M.C.A. man that I would attend to that. I was at work at this nearly all day. I did not do any of the packing myself, but I was trying my best to reach every man in our town, and I think I got everyone. Then too, I was trying to get a piano and stoves put into our Y.M.C.A. hall. That also was left on me. I feel sure that we shall get them in tomorrow morning, and open up tomorrow night. Also, I was trying to cudgel up out of my dusty cobwebbed cranium material for a Christmas talk. All the men got their packages, each containing a cigar, a cake of chocolate, and two packages of cigarettes or one of cakes. We had a good service with almost all the battalion in attendance. And after that a real good movie. So, as a whole, the day was as pleasant as Christmas in Rhineland could easily be made for our men. I had better luck with my Christmas exercises than our Chaplain had. He was thoroughly discouraged this morning, Chaplain Lewis said. My work for the last few days has reminded me very much of my work in Kelly Field. That kind of work, as you know, is no new thing to me. But it tries my patience just as much as it ever did.

I am not going to receive any commission. It cannot be done now. I don't care much. The application should have gone in earlier. I had plenty of time to get it before the armistice was declared. I have a letter from Mr. Reese, though, that I am going to keep. Maybe, I'll show it to you some day.

. . .

I stopped writing for just a few minutes to go into a saloon in the next room. Are you astonished? Don't be surprised at anything that I may do. However, this time I went in to glean something that might prove interesting reading, whether written in an interesting manner or not. It is an ordinary wine room. More often over here they are called cafes. It is a rare thing though that you see a German drunk. It is also true that very little strong drink is bought. So a saloon over here is not quite so disrespectable as in the States. I have not yet been able to determine, or decide, for myself whether it is less injurious. Understand, all my evidence is by observation, and none by actual experience. People over here drink wine and beer during all their waking hours. Indeed, it is a part of their food. And I don't know whether they ever drink water. In this particular saloon at present there is little standing room. Almost all the customers are civilians, and of these quite a few are women and girls. Everyone has a glass before him, of wine or beer. The women and girls drink too. The men do not pull their hats off. They are not nearly so courteous to women as Americans are, and women over here do things for men that girls in the U.S. would never think of doing. For example, every morning when a man appears on the streets, even though there is always mud and slush, his boots or shoes are always clean and neatly shined. I have never yet seen a man cleaning his heavy muddy shoes, but I have often seen women doing this work of the bootblack. It's pretty soft though for the man. I don't know how it would make me feel every morning to find my shoes neatly shined for the new day by my landlady or her daughter. Everyone seems to be talking in the wine-room and occasionally the mingled laughter of men and women is heard, rather loud and boisterous, I must say, and not at all like a party of normal Americans. Also the tobacco smoke is so thick you could cut it with a knife, and the smell is as strong as the inevitable front door decorations and ornament of every French, and almost every German home. One woman said to us, after tasting her wine, "Nicht gut." She said she did not like it. I think that the best class of people do not have this custom. But all, men, women, and children, drink wine in the home.

The Germans are going to have an election January nineteenth, but I am afraid it will not clarify the muddle in Germany to any great degree. The people, a German told Chaplain Lewis and me this afternoon, have been deceived so long that they do not know now when they are being lied to or when they are told the truth. This German further went on to say that for the first time ever known the wealthy class and the church are lined up together to put in the Centrist (Catholic section of the Reichstag, you know). Heretofore, the wealthy people have held aloof from the church, but now their interests are threatened by the Social Democrats, who, while of no declared religious attitude, are more and more opposing all religions. And quite externally and inevitably too. For, as always in the history of labor in other countries, the church, Catholic and Protestant, is opposing the Social Democrats. There is considerable agitation in certain quarters for the separation of the church from the state and also from the school. Until the evil influence of the state church in education and civil affairs is ended, it will be difficult to make any real reforms, I believe. In the present contest, the "pastors" are covertly telling the people that if they do not vote for a certain class of men, they will all be lost and go to hell. The Germans said this of the Catholic Church. He said all the women are going to vote as the priests wanted them to. (The women are going to vote in this election, too, you see.) This German, and others with him, said that the great part of the strong middle class was destroyed in the war and now there remain only the wealthy and the lowest classes. He said many Germans would leave after the war and go to the Americas. Almost all of them have relatives in the U.S., and they ask us if we know them.

Myrtle, do you realize that seven months have passed since that day which meant, and means, so much to us? Viewed in one way, it seems, oh, so distant and remote. But in another it seems very near. I can never forget some of the incident of that day. Do you remember those moments outside on the porch? It was there that I knew how much you loved me. And you answered my question there before I asked you later upstairs, how fast those moments passed! And since then we have had no chance to talk and plan for the future. Won't we have lots to talk about when we meet again? My own dear girl, I have many plans and I know you have too. It won't be so very many months until we shall talk about those plans to our hearts' content. Know that I love you with an ever growing love. You will mean more and more to me as the months pass by, and your influence and your help, and you, will make my life better, stronger, and more unselfish, as we are with each other more. I know that I shall always love you and it will always give me pleasure to show this feeling either in doing something for you or by some expression of affection. I am waiting too for the time when I shall see tokens of your love for me. I am almost ashamed to say it, but I was never so hungry in my heart for the expressed affection of human beings. Every child I see I would like to hold in my arms. And I am not the only one either.

As ever, dearest Myrtle,

Yours,

Eugene

Letter 25: December 29, 1918

My own dearest Myrtle,

It is raining tonight and it gives everyone a rather lonely feeling. I am still at the Y.M.C.A., as it is the most spiritual place that I can find for doing my writing. There is no stove in my room and I have to search around the best I can for a place in which to spend my idle moments. I am usually pretty busy during the day, though I must say I accomplish nothing so far as I can see. I spend some of my leisure moments in battalion headquarters but I hate to loaf around there too much, as the major may think I should be elsewhere at work. He is good to all his men, and if a man gets a reprimand from him, he (the man) may be quite certain that he deserved it.

. . . These Sundays are becoming harder and harder for me. I want to get back to Edna, to my work and friends, and to you. You don't know how much of my time my thoughts are of you. That and thoughts of Mamma and the rest are the greatest pleasures of my life now . . . Never can I forget the night of the twenty fifth of April and also of May. I learned a lot that was highly pleasing to me that night. It was then that I found out how much you thought of me. Since then you have meant more and more and will mean more to me as the days pass.

Dear, I am telling, since sitting here and at the same time as I write, one of my friends of our engagement, and of that happy day that will some day in the distant future come to us two. I do not tell your name. He does not think of that. Most of the boys over here are engaged, and so it is not so exciting to learn of an engagement as back home. I have not told anyone of our engagement. At least I have not told who the unfortunate (?) damsel is. But I am debating whether I shall tell Mamma or not. Sometimes I think I shall. Then again I decide not to. But there is plenty of time yet to decide that.

We have big reports of the reception that is being prepared for our brigade. It is known as "The Texas Brigade," as most of the men are from Texas. Many of the men are from Houston and they get news of preparations for the homecoming. For my own part parades and other such antics might be dispensed with. But I readily appreciate the spirit which prompts them. However, it may not take so very long to run the gantlet. It would tickle me very much if I could get a short leave while we are in Houston and make a flying trip to Edna. That is too much to hope for. And besides all this parade stuff may be only rumor. We have rumors flying around every day of the date set for our sailing, but so far all of them have been only rumors.

. . . I am in my room now . . . I went downstairs to see if I could locate the hydrant. But the lady of the house saw me with the pitcher and she said something about "forgetting the water." (You see I am picking up German right along. It is not so hard.) She usually wants to try to talk, but tonight I was glad to hear her say "Gente Nocht" without any other jabbering.

We have quite a time making ourselves understood. She knows some Latin and she has a son who speaks French with just about as little fluency as I do. But by combining French, Latin, and German we manage to carry on a rather unsatisfactory conversation occasionally.

. . .

She took me through their church yesterday. As she is an extremely devout Catholic, I was quite surprised when she asked such a great heretic as a Protestant minister must in the nature of the case be, to view their church. It is a large church and very beautiful inside. The stained glass windows are wonderful. She conducted me around to the contribution box. She finally made me understand that it was for missions in Africa. I dropped in fifteen pfennigs. According to prewar values that was the heartbreaking seen of about four cents. Now it is not more than two cents and a half. The mark has hit the toboggan and doesn't seem to be able to put on the brakes. I would have thrown in more, but, as a matter of fact, I had only a half franc besides and I did not want to be entirely bankrupt. (Last night I had a payday and received pay for my labor since September first. Pay for August was the last I had received. So you can imagine how lean my old pocketbook is.) In one window was a hole, a souvenir of an air raid here last spring. Nine bombs were dropped. The first one, rather curiously, cut the main light wire and threw the whole town into the darkness. That saved the town. Three bombs fell in the street, one hit and demolished a dwelling and the others hit in an apple orchard that is almost in town. Three civilians were killed and a few injured.

. . .

It is getting late and Brady has already "hit the hay," or feathers rather, I believe I'll follow suit.

My love is yours,

Eugene

Letter 26: December 31, 1918

My dearest Myrtle,

I have just come back from my second trip to Graach today to see Chaplain Lewis. And both times I failed. Graach is a small village across and up the Moselle. The second battalion of the 360th is quartered there and Chaplain Lewis is trying to help them in the straight and narrow path. It is almost a mile from here and I had to make my last trip just after supper.

An order came to me from regimental this afternoon ordering me to report at once for duty as assistant to the regimental chaplain. So I went over tonight to report. But I couldn't, for Chaplain Lewis was still absent. He went to Trier yesterday and has not yet returned. I am considerably puzzled as to what this order means. Several times heretofore there have been hints or suggestions that I be transferred to some other organization. But I had always been able to avert it. I have been with the first battalion so long and know so many friends here that the idea of going elsewhere is not particularly appealing to me. It has been done by the Colonel's order too. However, I can only carry it out fully, and I have already tried to do that.

This order has left me up in the air as to planning any services for tomorrow. It is New Year's, you see, and I wanted to have some kind of a service at sometime during the day. As it is, it is impossible to plan anything. I may be in another town by this time tomorrow and attached to another organization. Such is life in the army though. Probably there will be nothing at all here.

. . .

How many resolutions have you made for the New Year? So far I have made only one. I am seriously thinking of cancelling it before the new year begins. It may inconvenience me in the future.

Write as often as you can. Your letters mean much to me over here. It always makes me feel good to get one from you.

As ever, with love,

Eugene

Letter 27: January 4, 1919

My dearest Myrtle,

. . .

The bugler is blowing "Taps." I like to hear "Taps" blown. It seems to me to be an appropriate conclusion to the soldier's day. When we were back in Luxemburg, we had a regular military funeral at the death of a soldier who died there from natural causes. The last thing in a military funeral is the blowing of "taps" over the soldier's grave. We had a good bugler and he blew it so soft and low and feelingly. It is supposed to be blown at the burial of every soldier, but on the battlefield of course that was impossible. I never had anything more than a short simple prayer. One time I started to read a passage but had not finished the first verse when a whizz-bang bursted over us. I saw that I would soon be alone, so I followed the others. There was no use to risk any more lives anyway. That was on the San Mihiel salient on Hill 327. Perhaps you have read something about it. There are many interesting incidents connected with it. They must keep for a while yet though.

. . .

I am sending you a memorandum which has been sent to every man in the brigade. It shows something of the part taken by this brigade in the great struggle. I have marked those places which I know certainty to have been taken by the 360 Inf. Hill 327 was the hardest of all. It cost us heavily, but it will live in immortal glory. The spirit shown on that hill is unsurpassable. But I won't tell you about it now. Please save this memorandum. I would not lose it for quite a bit. It is one souvenir that I want to keep.

. . .

With lots of love, I am, as ever,

Yours,

Eugene

Letter 28: January 7, 1919

My dearest Myrtle,

Just two years and a half ago today I moved myself and all of my baggage into Edna. It seems impossible that the time has passed so quickly. And, on the other hand, it seems that so much could have been compressed into so short a time. There have been so many changes, so many varieties of work, and so many lasting and deep impressions and experiences. If the years to come furnish as varied a program, I am afraid that I shall end up at the North Pole, or in some other unthought of place.

Seriously, I can hardly realize that so much has been encompassed within so short a time. The first period was most important to me because it marked the real beginning at last of my lifework, and the finding of so many good friends in Edna. Those first months held days of agony for me. What's more, I am afraid that many of the experiences only agonizing in degree, will have to be repeated when I begin again. For you must realize that it will be a new beginning. Many of my old sermons will be 'scrapped.'

Then there came the war with its complex calls. First was the Y.M.C.A., and later real soldiering as a buck private. I don't suppose I shall ever be able to calculate how much I have been changed during these months. But everyone has been changed equally as much and perhaps more. It will take some time for all of us to classify these new ideas and impressions and select those which are permanent and right.

Dear Myrtle, one of the most pleasant features of these months has been the association with you. My pleasantest memories are those that are connected with you. I have learned to love you, and to love you with all my heart. Some of those incidents will live in my mind forever.

I am getting cold and my fingers are numb. Will finish later.

. . .

You had not heard from me when you wrote me last. That is, a letter written after the 11th. Perhaps some of the uneasiness you all felt for the boys over here on the Meuse front was real. It was one more battle, believe me. But I was in no danger. You know all about it though from your letters that I have written since November 11th.

. . .

My hostess (?) and her son had quite a scene last night. The first I knew of it was when a friend of mine came and asked me if I would go into the house with him. The son was acting crazy and his mother was afraid to go in. We went in and found him in the kitchen, cooking some Irish potatoes. He did not attempt to injure us or his mother. Another American came in, who could speak German. He tried to reconcile them, but all in vain. The mother would not agree, although the son was quite willing. She was trying to tell me something about it today. She was so stirred up about it then that she could not entirely keep the tears back, proud as she was. I think her patience has been worn out. The son is a lazy, ill, good-for-nothing sort of fellow. She said today that he has never worked any. She is a widow and works all the time. He must have used force, as she mentioned a red ear which he had given her. Today he left and I expect it is for the best. He carouses around all night and then wants the house quiet so he can sleep in the day time. He is "buggy," I think she says he is "sick in the head." Don't doubt it either.

Several days ago she was telling me about the scarcity of cotton. It is impossible to buy it now at all. She showed me linen sheets that her mother knitted forty or more years ago. I was surprised. These were on my bed. Soap can't be bought either. They have a soap made out of a kind of fine soft stone which they use. It is not very satisfactory though.

. . .

Eugene

[The following pages out of order, may
be misplaced, enclosed with letter 28]

. . .

Only one letter came to me today, but it has been a long time since any letter has made me feel so good as this one has. It is your Christmas letter to me. The contents of the letter are fine. But I value those pictures a lot more. You don't know how glad I was to see that one from you. You would be embarrassed, I suspect, if you knew how much I have looked at it today. It is the first time I have seen a picture of you in about seven months. I am sincerely glad to get it. It will be frequently consulted in the days to come. It is a good picture of you and quite natural. I shall be glad to see that smile on the original. This picture and the letter have made me more homesick than ever. When, oh when? That is the all-important question. Everyday finds everyone of us more anxious to take the back trail.

. . .

Chaplain Lewis asked me today for a list of the men whom I buried on the last drive. I had the names of one hundred and three. He had about the same number, or perhaps more. These were all Americans. In addition to these, I buried about sixty Germans. We buried enemy dead as well as our own.

Two letters came to me today asking for details concerning the deaths of two boys. One is from a mother and the other from a brother. Such letters are always coming in. I answered one yesterday about a boy that was killed about the 19th or 20th of September. This is only one of the many sad aftermaths of war.

Letter 29: January 12, 1919

My dearest Myrtle,

. . .

You would never guess what kind of work I am doing now, in addition to what I have already. I suppose you would call me battalion school superintendent. This has just been wished off on me. As a matter of fact, an officer is supposed to be dedicated especially for this work, but so many of the officers of our battalion are away at short-course military schools that no officer is at present available for our local school work. As soon Lt. Gray gets back, I want to give up my new job. I would work just as hard with him in charge. Besides, he is an experienced school man, having been county superintendent in the states.

It is difficult to tell whether the schooling will amount to anything or not. We can appropriate from the Germans their school buildings, blackboards, etc. But it may be difficult to secure the proper textbooks, although the order says they will be available in a short time. Class will be started at once in reading, writing, and speaking English, and also in arithmetic, without textbooks. Classes in geography, U.S. history, French, etc., will be begun just as soon as the proper textbooks arrive. I am not to do any of the teaching, according to present plans. Later on, I may have to give some lectures (so called) on civics. How do you think you would like to teach one of these classes? I can give you a "job" all right. It is ordered that "instructors are released from all other military duties." Drilling is the principal occupation at present during the day. The school will be held at night. Come over and help me. What I don't know about school work would run into volumes. You could fill up a lot of my deficiencies.

. . .

We had services this morning at the Y.M.C.A. here. Only about forty or fifty were present. It was not announced at the companies, so only a few of them knew about it. Chaplain is going to talk tonight. Neither he nor Chaplain Byrnes ever attempted two services for their organizations, but I have had pretty good luck so far. So I think I shall continue two services each Sunday.

It is unbounded vanity or conceit perhaps on my part, but I am nearly crazy to get back into the work of a pastorate. I like to talk, especially if I know that I have something that is worth listening to. When I get settled down again, I want to work out a schedule of study and reading. There is much hard work ahead of me, if I do what I want to do, and I am going to try to have some system about it. You have heard me say that one of your hardest tasks would be to help me at work. But that is exactly what you must do. You remember too what Miss Murphy said one day at dinner when she was in Edna last. Your work is pretty well cut out for you, I think.

Just a year ago today I was in Edna . . . Today is just such a day as it was that Saturday when Mrs. Arthur met me at the train. We went straight to Mr. Jim Power's for Mrs. Power's funeral. It sure was cold. You, I recall, were perched up before the fire, sick or at least afraid to brave the disagreeable weather.

Do you remember what we did that last night? I have often thought about it, and without the least regret too. When our hands were together during prayers, I wondered what you were thinking of me, and I have wondered since. I shall be glad when we are together again. We understand each other fully now and we won't be wondering what the other is thinking about us. I never did worry very much, because I knew you loved me before you knew it, I believe. I know that I loved you long before I ever said that I did.

. . .

I have been thinking of you lots today, dear, and wishing to be with you, if only for a few minutes. You may be absolutely sure that my love is growing stronger for you all the time.

Love to you, my own dear Myrtle, with all my heart.

Lovingly yours,

Eugene

Letter 30–31: January 15, 1919

My own dearest Myrtle,

. . .

I am a "prof." these days, I suppose. At any rate, I am all mixed up with this school business. We have fine classes going. Most of the members of these classes are really interested too. Illiterates and foreign-speaking men are compelled to attend. What do you suppose I am teaching? You would never guess. I have a class of three, no, four, Mexicans who do not understand a word of English. One of them can write and read Spanish. The others never had such an idea. But I am teaching them reading, writing, and speaking English all at one time. Although I have had only two lessons, they do fine. They want to learn. I took the class more as an experiment that anything else. Then, too, I could not find a teacher for it. As soon as I find a teacher, I am going to surrender my promising pupils.

Two of the teachers have had several years of experience in teaching in Texas. However, at times, I am surprised at some of their methods. I had to call them down on holding classes too long. One of them tonight galloped on his all-fours before a class who can neither read nor write to show them what a certain word meant. Last night he was giving to the class the sound of a certain letter. Then he said to all the class, "Emulate me!" Perhaps it is a good suggestion. Do you school your pupils 'to emulate' you? They would have an excellent paragon all right. But emulation of one's self must be encouraged very diplomatically.

. . .

Since I am on this line, I had just as well tell one on myself. We have been selling canned soup at the Y.M.C.A. lately. The other day I decided to heat a can and try it. It was Campbell's Tomato Soup. You have seen it advertised, I know. I heated it on the stove and then carried it back into the supply room to cut it open and eat it. I stuck a hole in it with my knife with the intention of pouring it out into a pasteboard box. But as soon as a hole was made the thing began to steam and sputter worse than a steam engine. Apparently there was too much in there. Before I could get it at a safe distance, it had given a distinct tomato shade to my face and a little went on my blouse. I turned it away at another angle. It decorated the ceiling, wall, and window beautifully. Also a table came in for its share. I had a real job of cleaning up the window and my face. I thought sure my face was blistered. But it is not so bad. I lost more than half of the soup. The other was good though. I have not heated any more soup in the can.

. . .

Letter 32: January 20, 1919

My dearest Myrtle,

You will doubtless be surprised when you hear of my good fortune. I have been granted a three days leave of absence to visit Paris. That is, I shall have the privilege of spending seventy-two hours in the world's greatest city. Only two men in the battalion received passes. So you can see how fortunate I was. I am [in] Trier (or Treves) waiting for a train to take me to Metz. The battalion sergeant major is with me. Our train leaves at eleven-forty five. I have something over an hour in which to write.

We are in a Red Cross station. It is maintained for just such men as the sgt-maj and me. It would be cold and distinctly unpleasant to have to wait in a cold room. This is my first experience with the Red Cross in this kind of work. I have seen its work on and near the battlefield and it is just as good here. When we arrived here, we were rather cold from a long ride. We came into this room, which is a part of the railroad station, and found a pot of steaming coffee and cups on a counter. Also several varieties of sandwiches. I have made five or six trips already. Such things are appreciated when a soldier is on leave. He would have a hard time holding body and soul together, as we are not allowed to buy anything at all from the Germans.

We hear all kinds of rumors as to how soon we are to start home. The latest is that we sail early in March. That means the division must soon be on the move. I left all my equipment at Wehlen. I am in hopes the battalion will be gone when I get back. I could soon catch it. Anyway, I did not want to be bothered with a pack and other impediments on a leave. I did bring some German field glasses. I was afraid they might find a new owner in my absence. I stuck them in my pocket and intend to keep them until I am safe in the States. I prize them very highly, as they are of good grade. I showed them to a German optician the other day and he said they were made in the best factory in Germany. I picked them up on the morning of November first.

Last Thursday I went through an old castle on a hill near Berncastel. It was extremely interesting and doubtless has an equally interesting history. It commanded a view of the Moselle Valley in both directions and also several valleys leading out of the Moselle. It was typical of its age and time. Of course only the walls remain today. The castle tower is by far the most interesting part of the old ruins. It is perhaps eighty or more feet high. Its diameter is between thirty six and forty feet. At the bottom the walls are about fourteen feet thick, but up toward the top they are thinner. Even there the walls are thick enough to contain a circular staircase and still have about five feet of stone and mortar between you and the outside wall. There was also the dungeon in the tower. It's only opening was from above. I could not get into this section. A rope would have been necessary. It could easily be seen that a prisoner or valuables would be equally safe in its keeping. I was especially anxious to see this part of the castle and explore it, but I was disappointed. I was afraid to try to crawl in there and out again. I might have ended my roseate prospects in a sudden tragic death.

While in Paris I hope to get a glimpse of some of the famous men in the Peace Conference. I am especially anxious to see our President. He is far and away the biggest man in the world today. He has won a big victory for himself and America over here. Americans over here even don't appreciate him at his true worth, and they are more generous in their praise than the papers back home. At least, those any I have had the good fortune to get my hands on. The English press is lavish in its praise of him. It will take several decades to appraise him at his correct value.

He is a big man, though, and every American ought to be thankful for such a fellow-citizen.

Lot of love. I would like to write more. Maybe I shall find time. Always as I have been.

Your own,

Eugene

Letter 34: February 18, 1919

My own dearest Myrtle,

. . .

I got a letter from you today. If you had any idea as to the effect upon me of a single letter from you. You would never consider any of them wasted. It does me good in more ways than I can tell. Or, rather, it is difficult for me to describe its full effect on me. Your letters always make me happy, not as happy as I could be or would like to be by any means, but they make me feel much better. I wish I could get one every day while I am in this God-forsaken country. You have no idea how discouraged we become at times over here. It seems almost unendurable. A letter at such times is simply a God-given word of comfort or encouragement.

. . .

In today's letter you ask if it is true that the greater part of the M.G.Co. 360 Inf. was killed or wounded and the remainder transferred. I have often wanted to express myself on this subject, but it always slipped my mind at the time I was writing. That boy's neck ought to be twisted good and hard. I mean the one who wrote the article to that Post to the effect that the Machine Gun Company had been almost wiped out of existence. In comparison with the infantry companies, their losses were light. The official percentage of losses, as given out by regimental, was 66% for the first battalion. The strength of the M.G.Co. was 132 on Nov. 15. They lost 42 out of 172 men, the total strength of the company. This was killed and wounded and, was official. Their loss then was practically 25%. So you can see that report was a wild exaggeration. I can't understand why a sensible person should start such a thing. It caused untold worry in this case. I always minimized, if I could not represent things as they actually were. For example, the artillery fire on the San Mihiel front was terrific. But I never did write it that way. What good would it have done?

. . .

I laughed loud and long when I came to the part of your letter where you asked me if I ever dined out. No, not yet. I don't expect to pull such an amazing stunt until I get back in the States. I don't want to eat out over here in Germany. You remember that in some of my letters I spoke of the seemingly sincere change of the Germans. I was uncertain then. I am not uncertain now. From my experience and observation, I know that they have not changed. In fact, it was too much to expect them to change so quickly and so completely. They are just as consciousless as ever. And I would not eat at a German's table, with its evident avowal of friendship and comradeship for the whole world, not though it was a feast fit for a king. They have not changed and that is what makes me bitter against them. I had a much more Christian, or at least friendly, feeling for them on Nov. 11 than I have now. We want to be just, but we must be firm and unbending, if our victory is to be permanent.

Didn't I ever write you about the Meuse fight? I thought sure I had written that long ago. It is such a long story that I am afraid I would prefer not to write it anyway. All that I could do, would be to describe what I saw and heard. That would be only a small part of what actually took place. I'll think about it.

The Germans here have had two weddings recently. One took place only yesterday. The ceremony took place in the church. I did not see that, although many of the boys did. After that, a procession formed with the newly married couple leading, and marched to the home of the bride, I think. The bride was dressed in black, with the conventional bridal head gear of some white gossamer-like fabric. A little girl dressed in white acted as train-bearer, I suppose, you would call it. The groom was dressed in black too. Prince Albert coat, high silk hat, etc. The other groom, of about three weeks ago now, was one-eyed. The blushing bride had most of her front teeth gone. In the afternoon they formed another procession and paraded the town. I understand that this was for the purpose of showing off the bride gown. It is interesting as a spectator, but I would not want to be one of the two principle actors.

Lot and lots of love, my own dear girlie.

Yours devotedly,

Eugene

The city of
Luxemburg

The 360th Infantry
crossed into Germany
by this bridge over
the Moselle River on
December 6, 1918,
for occupation duty.

Castle at Bernkastel, Germany

90th Division bakery at Bernkastel; photograph courtesy World War I
Signal Corps photograph collection, U.S. Army Heritage and Education Center

YMCA Hall in Wehlen, Germany

Letter 35: February 25, 1919

My dearest Myrtle,

. . .

I got a letter today from Mr. Rogers, telling me of Ben's death and asking me to find out any details of his death, burial, etc. It was quite a shock to me to learn of his death. He was one of my best friends among the Edna boys. I shall do all I can. At most, that won't be much . . .

Letters of inquiry in regard to the death of relatives reach me every week. It is trying to me to have to send back so little. I have been working for the last two weeks on the records of the dead in this regiment. I am trying to gather all the information I can in case these letters come. Often the details of a man's death are meager. Sometimes none of the circumstances is known. The homefolks want every little bit of information, and so also do the friends or relatives over here. We have had four communications from a lieutenant in the A.E.F. whose brother Chap. Lewis and I buried. I must write a letter tomorrow to a girl whose brother was in this battalion. He was a company runner and was killed on the morning of November 1. Two other runners were killed and five other men were wounded by one shell. I was able to find a boy who was there at the time. So I can give her a little more information than usual in such cases.

Dying by shellfire or from a bullet is not like a death brought about by disease or some other cause working in a natural way. In battle men were killed instantly. There was no parting word, no suffering. It was over in less than a second.

Brady has the "homesickness" blues tonight. He has just gone up and gone to bed. I never saw so many homesick men in all my life. It is almost alarming. Let me tell you a joke on Brady. For some time he has been complaining about not getting letters from his "girl." Last week he learned the 'wherefore' of it. He has been writing to two girls. Naturally, he, or the censor, (he says the censor is to blame) exchanged letters and the right envelopes carried the wrong letters to the wrong girls. Lately he has been under a barrage of drumfire intensity. He is hopelessly defeated and has withdrawn his attack at both points.

. . .

Lots and lots of love, my own Myrtle, and remember that my heart's love is yours.

Your own,

Eugene

Letter 36: March 5, 1919

My own dearest Myrtle,

. . . I am far behind with my correspondence and several days ago I laid aside a copy of the "Stars and Stripes" that had the covenant of the League of Nations in it. I can't know whether my limited mental powers can take in its full and exact meaning. Everyone, even a "buck private," should know enough about it to carry on an intelligible discussion about the league, though.

It seems that the League of Nations is the topic of all discussions in America, according to our news over here. Of course, as a soldier in the U.S. Army, I am not supposed to have an opinion or even a mind of my own. Still, I can't keep from being interested in such a far-reaching issue as the League of Nations. I hope Wilson and the American people put it over and put it over 'big.' It is the only untried remedy of the many that have been put forward to abolish war, or at least make it almost impossible. It should be given a chance at any rate. All the others have had their chance and have failed . . . I sometimes wonder whether those people who are most bitter against the league had ever seen the destructiveness of war on a battlefield, would oppose the idea of world league to prevent war.

. . . The people here are doing lots of work in the vineyards these days. They go out early and come back for dinner, and then go again. Women and girls do a lot of the pruning. Most of the men pack fertilizer up these steep hills on their backs. It is hard heavy work. They carry from ninety to a hundred and twenty-five pounds at each trip. For a day's work they receive four marks and fifty pfennigs. This is for the heaviest work. The pruners get about three and sometimes as much as three and a half or four marks. The average, I suppose is about three and a half marks. The pre-war value of the mark was between twenty three and twenty four cents. They always bundle up the cuttings and bring these home, to use them for fuel, I suppose. The people are extremely poor and have absolutely no prospect here, at least under the old regime. Let us hope that the new order of things will change the lot of the mass of the German population. It is wretched in the extreme.

Today is Ash Wednesday, a fast day over here, and, indeed, among all Roman Catholics. The lady of the house here has just gone to the church. She seemed rather surprised when she learned that we did not observe it as such. I have less and less respect for the results of their religion over here. In fact, I can't see any noticeable results. They have lots of prayer books, but no Bibles. Shrines are everywhere, but they are without worshippers. They have frequent services at the church, but like our own Christianity, their practice falls far short. I can't quite understand their idea of religion over here. The erection of the shrines along the roads, or hillsides, and in every conceivable place is certainly prompted by some worthy notice, but what is its practical value? I have yet to see a person make even the sign of the cross as he passes one. The only use that I have seen is that of sheltering a bunch of workmen in some of the severe weather. Indeed many of the shrines seem to be loafing places. The wine is kept warm by a fire on the rock floor and is frequently tasted. No one over here, of the natives I mean, drinks water. Even this old lady here made a wry face when I told her that I never drank anything but water and coffee.

Several Germans have died in Wehlen lately. Most of them were influenza—pneumonia cases. Their food is of such poor quality and little quantity that their bodies have little power of resistance against any disease. Many are dying all over Germany and I suspect under nutrition is the cause of almost all of it. But they have only themselves to blame.

. . . Please tell me how you are standing the school work, and all about yourself. I love you with all my heart and anything that concerns you is of interest to me.

Lots and lots of love.

Your own,

Eugene

I am enclosing a copy of a communication from Chaplain Reese to the assistant Chief of staff of the 90th Div. Chaplain Reese sent me a carbon copy which I want to keep, but I am afraid I may lose it in my wanderings. I would like to keep a copy just as evidence of what I did "in the war." Bye Bye, Eugene

P.S. While I am sending this copy, I had just as well include some other things.

One is our division insignia, "representing Texas + Oklahoma." Someone has jestingly said it stands for "Texas Thieves and Oklahoma Outlaws." All combat divisions, as you doubtless know, have special distinctive insignia worn on the left arm of the top of the sleeve.

I am also sending you a poem written by one of the boys in the medical detachment assigned to our battalion. While the division was in the Argonne, he was attached to "A" company. On "Hill 327" this company was reduced to a combat strength of twenty six rifles. The company had been ordered to take a certain objective absolutely essential for the safety of the remainder of the battalion. Across a valley a few hundred yards away was a Prussian machine gun battalion and they didn't fail to use their guns. Our men dug "fox holes" as quickly as possible but they did not have the proper implements. But they were exposed to a flank as well as frontal fire and the result was that almost the whole company was lost. They sacrificed themselves for the safety of the other companies of the battalion. Some of the most stirring deeds I have known or heard of during all the war occurred in this fight. The captain, second in command, and top sergeant were all killed early in the fight. But other noncoms did the work splendidly. Even privates alone would have held the position. A reserve battalion of Prussian guards counter-attacked, but by the time they had advanced to within fifty yards of Co. A. all their officers had fallen and they retreated. If they had continued their advance, Co. A would have been wiped out of existence. Twenty six men out of the company were killed here and no one knows how many were wounded. The twenty six men are buried in one grave in order of rank, the captain first, lieutenant second, top sergeant third, etc. The attack was made in the afternoon and so many were wounded that it was impossible to remove them to the first aid station. Those able gathered blankets and relived the suffering as much as possible. But many died from exposure, as it was very cold and was really raining. Not many men could be spared from the front line as they were few enough at best and a counter attack was bound to come, as in fact it did. It was a terrible night, but such a night as had many parallels during the war.

There is a companion piece to this one in praise of the lieutenant who was sent by Maj. Morris to take command of Co. A. His name is Lt. Gary, from Falfurrias, or at any rate, from that section. He was a school teacher before the war came on. As a man, I have not seen his superior in the army, nor even perhaps his equal.

I could write almost a book on "Hill 327," but I must wait and tell you. It is too long a story.

Eugene

Letter 37: March 12, 1919

My own dear Myrtle,

A man from Chicago, Illinois has just given us a splendid talk. He has been in Europe only a short time. Being such a recent arrival from that "glory land," he is intensely interesting. His subject tonight was "The Man for the Times." It was very practical and gave us something of the conditions back home and how we must be qualified if we are to help meet those conditions.

This has been a full day with me, although I don't see anything that I have actually done. That is the way with all my days. They pass by and although I am running around and about a lot, nothing very much worth while seems to have been done.

Chaplain Lewis has left the regiment and is now pursuing studies in the University of Paris. He did not appeal to me very much when he first came to us, but the more I knew him, the better I liked him. I certainly did hate to see him go. He is gone for good, I am almost sure. Of course, if we get to stay in this country until July or August he will probably come back to us. He has certainly been a friend to me. He has done more for me than anybody else in the army.

My landlady has just told me of the death of a man from tuberculosis today. He lives near here. She says that many people in this valley die of tuberculosis. She attributes it to the hard work in the vineyards. It is heavy work, "schwer arbeite," they call it, and no American soldier disagrees with them. They have vineyards only on the steepest hills, you might almost say cliffs. They are the next thing to cliffs. Men and boys, and sometimes women and girls I am told, although I have never actually seen them, carry soil, crushed rock, and heavy wet barnyard fertilizer up these steepest slopes on their backs. Then of course the grapes, at harvest time, have to be brought down. This woman says eventually their chest sinks in, or breaks. I could not quite understand what he meant. Girls of fourteen are regular workers during the busy seasons. At this particular time of the year they may be hurrying to and from their work. They are dressed in coarse rough clothing, wear heavy shoes, and carry their pruning shears in their hand. These girls all suffer from working in the vineyards, she says.

Guess what I did today, among the many things that I filled up the day with. I packed in a little tin box some souvenirs of this old continent, to Mrs. Arthur a flashlight that I found on November first on the Argonne sector, and,—but this sentence would become too long. If my recollection serves me right, Bess had somewhat mutilated her napkin-holder, or-ring. One day when I was in Norroy, I picked up a napkin-ring and am sending it to her. Some coins for Howe and Ruth and a whetrock for Hawley are also in it. The coins are self explanatory. I found the rock in the Argonne and have carried it in my pocket ever since.

To you, I am sending a doily(?) I suppose you would call it. Anyway it is needlework. I bought it in Virton, Belgium. My judgement of needle-work is untried, so don't be surprised if it is not good work. I suppose the material was as good as they could get under the circumstances.

I am also sending you, in another package, some views of this country. One album is entitled "Die Eifel." It is a series of reproductions from original paintings of an upland district called "The Eifel." These repro-ductions are remarkable, I think. Another album contains views of the Moselle from Coblence to Trier, or Treves. I hope both packages arrive safely at their destination.

. . .

My dearest heart was never so hungry for love in all my life. You don't know how anxious I am to see you. I am much more anxious to see you than anyone else, although, God knows I am crazy to see anyone that I have ever known. I dreamed of you the other night and it was such a vivid dream. It seemed almost real. The look in your eyes and the smile on your face were as plain as on last May 20th. Almost ten months have passed and it will be several months yet before I can see you. How slow time goes! A few months seem almost an eternity.

Well, dearest, I must close. I am not at all blue this morning, al-though you might get that impression from this letter, I have written, though, what is deeper than the surface.

All my love is yours, darling, and God grant that we may soon see each other.

Yours devotedly,

Eugene

Letter 38a: March 13, 1919

My own Myrtle,

I got the sweetest letter this morning that I ever received. I have already read it six times and I don't know how many times more I shall read it. And it came only two hours ago at that. It is almost as sweet as you are, dear. That would be, in the language of culture, going some.

We are having a half holiday. I want to do some writing. I have done a variety of things already. I have made two intrusions into what is considered distinctly women's sphere. First of all I did some sewing. Can you imagine me with a needle in my fingers? It was clumsily done, but it will last as long as I am in the army. You did some sewing for me once, didn't you? You have doubtless forgot all about it. Then I had to do some washing. I can do that fine. I washed only one pair of trousers this afternoon. Last night I did a big washing though. I haven't much more love for it than Howe has. However, it was of necessity and not of choice. I'll try not to intrude any more often than I have to.

. . .

I am thankful for how you felt about His blessing on us last Sunday morning. I don't know why, but I have felt that presence increasingly in our relations. Why did neither of us feel that we were doing wrong in giving those little tokens of affection? If anyone had told me two years ago that I would have done such things, I would have scorned their word. But I never condemned myself, or you, a single time. There was a feeling in my heart that God was leading us closer together. (Don't think I am making Him responsible if there was any wrong in our acts.) He has certainly brought us together. And He will keep us together. I am hoping and earnestly praying. It is extremely pleasing to me to know that you think this as you do. It is another instance of your keeping concealed at ordinary time your really true and deepest thoughts. I hope He will give us many, many years together until our work is done.

. . .

I am so glad that you told me about how your love increased for me that morning while you were in my arms upstairs. It is sweet you say that you yearned to give me all your love and yourself. I wish I were with you long enough to express my appreciation of those words. I know I have the sweetest girl yet. It is your love and yourself that I want. It gives me great joy to think that both will be with me some day for all time.

My love for you was vastly stronger then than ever before. Do you remember my question while we were on the porch? When I knew what we each one thought about each other in regard to the other, I resolved at once to settle the question. That was why I asked you if you would come upstairs. I don't think I would have asked you to come up in order to say goodbye . . . I am extremely thankful that it is all settled now, except the best part of living out, in the years ahead of us, our promises. Our love will grow all the stronger. I like to think that my years are to be spent with you. And I gladly give myself to you for your happiness. If loving and serving and working in love will make you happy, I shall do my best to make you so. I want to do things for you. It is always easier for me to show or do, than to speak, and it is the same way with regard to my love for you. I shall be content when I make you content. Would it be saying too much to say that I shall do everything I can to make you happy? I don't think so, for the reason that you would never ask anything wrong or unreasonable. I have that much confidence in you. I know you will do absolutely what you think is right. My love wants to protect and care for you and love you all the days. Even that is not as much as you deserve or as much as I would like to give. I give it gladly to you, and myself with it.

. . .

My own dearest Myrtle,

. . .

Say, I am going to be really bossy. (You may be getting a forecast of the future(?)). I want you to quit calling me "Mr. McLaurin." It simply doesn't sound right to me. I want you to call me Eugene. I did not say "Miss Myrtle" a single time while I was in Edna. If you don't call me Eugene, I am going to call you Miss Myrtle, much as I dislike to. But I believe in equal rights and privileges for both. So please call me by my first name hereafter when we are together. You had just as well get accustomed to it, for you will have to call me that when we are married.

Dearest, to me it is a sweet thought to think that some day you and I shall be married. That word has an almost sacred meaning with me, and I mean it in its very highest sense.

. . .

Do you think, that I should have waited until some later time? I have thought that perhaps so soon after your grandfather's death was not the proper time. Yet I did not know when we would be together again. And the thought of death is constantly with us these days anyway. That is the only really terror of the war, but it spreads its gloom over everything. I wanted you to know, too, that I loved you with all my heart and soul and wanted to help you in your loss. I have always said that I would never propose by letter. It is 'tacky', I think, unless, indeed it is the only possible way.

. . .

Goodnight and pleasant dreams.

Yours,

Eugene

McLaurin returned to the U.S. aboard the troop ship USS Mongolia.

Letter 39: May 23, 1919

My own dearest Myrtle,

You are doubtless surprised at this heading, but have you been expecting the division to move so long that it does not surprise you? It hardly seems that we are on our way to home. We have left Germany at any rate and are in the western part of France.

We have been here three days now. We left Wengerohr, Germany, Saturday, May 17 at 6:69 P.M., and arrived in St. Nazaire Tuesday morning at ten o'clock. The trip was not so bad. Of course troops in Europe cannot have the accommodations of the U.S.A. But we got along much better than on that trip last July from Rochefort-sur-Mer to Recey-sur-Ource, down near Dijon. That was a long trip and we were thirty eight men to each of these "dinky" French cars. There were forty of us this last time, but we were in U.S.A. box cars and they are almost twice as long as the French cars. So we made it fairly well. We had bedsacks filled with shavings to sleep on and plenty to eat.

Time passes more slowly now than ever. We wander aimlessly around, trying to find a "timekiller," but it is a vain quest. I try to read, and have read several interesting articles and stories. But reading soon becomes tiresome and uninteresting. We don't have any work of any kind and the Y.M.C.A. furnishes entertainment only after supper. We are all so crazy to get home that we can't really do anything. Needless to say, I spend most of my waking hours thinking of the pleasure that the next few weeks will bring. That is an inexhaustible field for thought, but anticipation, compared with present conditions is rather depressing. We won't be satisfied though until we get home, and I sometimes wonder whether we will even then.

. . .

Influenza is certainly playing havoc in Edna. Davenport told me two days ago that Mrs. Grissom was dead. You wrote me about Mr. Staples and Mr. Raymond. A great many more have died at home than were killed at the front. I shall certainly miss a lot of those people. I can't realize yet that they are gone beyond recall. Mrs. Staples has my sympathy. I know she is almost prostrate. And I wonder what Jack Grissom will do with those children? He has tremendous responsibility for a man.

. . .

Myrtle, you can hardly realize how anxious I am to see you. It seems an age since I last saw you, almost one year ago. So many things have happened in that time. Both of us are changed in some ways at any rate. But I know that every change in me has only made my love for you stronger and surer. I don't know in what ways I have changed, but I am looking forward more and more to those days that I shall spend with you. Sometimes there is so much to be done and I am so little qualified to do a respectable share of it that I become discouraged. If it had not been for you and what you mean to me, I would not be coming home with the division. There is such a great need over here that I would have stayed longer. I confess that I was tempted to make a trial anyway. Don't become alarmed. I was not planning anything rash but there seemed to be so much work to be done over here and it will take Americans to do it. Or, at any rate, it can't be done by French or German. Don't say anything about what I have written in this paragraph, please. God knows, I want to see home and friends and get to work in America. But there is so much work to be done over here for Christ that it is enough to make a man a pessimist in his view of the final destiny of things and almost an unbeliever. It surpasses my comprehension to understand how any people could have been professed Christians for hundreds and hundreds of years without absorbing more of the real spirit of Christ and living a life more like his. It is beyond me.

You will think I am unsettled or indeed insane after having read the last paragraph, but I assure you I am not. I may as well tell you though as not that I have had my faith more severely tried in the last year than at any other time in my life. And it has not been so much on the battlefield either. But you are to be spared an account of the wanderings of my soul. Some of the questions that a man, any thinking human being, faces over here raises questions which he cannot solve satisfactorily or disregard. I only feel that "God's in His heaven, All's well with the world."

I have more faith than ever in Christ and I suppose I ought not to worry about His business over here. It is His and He is plenty able to take care of it. But it is a terrible mess at present, I can assure you without any exaggeration.

I am exceedingly anxious to get back to work. I have done nothing so long that I am afraid I shall still be a 'goldbricker' in spite of myself. It is going to be hard to get back to real good hard work.

Did you ever in your life read such a doleful pessimistic letter? I must have got up on the wrong side of the bed this morning, although, come to think about it, there was only one side that I could get out on. I shall try to turn to a more agreeable subject.

I am so glad that you are going to teach at Edna next year. I thought you would, but the thought came to me occasionally that you might have grown tired of Edna by this time. I wanted you to do what you wanted for yourself, and I was not saying a thing. But it gives me untold joy to know that next winter we shall be together. It almost pains me now to think of letting you get very far out of my sight. I want to be around you and see you around me. You have become very dear to me and my happiest hours are those that will be spent with you and for you. I would like to tell you how much I love you, but words seem hollow and lacking force. I love you with all my strength, with all that I am. You cannot know it now and it may be that you will never know how much I love you. The occasion for showing it fully may never arise. But it is there.

In six weeks at most, I shall be with you. I wonder where I shall see you first. I even wonder what kind of a dress you will be wearing. Would you have thought it? I pay attention to dresses, even though I am a man. It will be unutterable joy to be with you again. I also wonder when our first long talk will take place. It is so hard to wait for all these things.

Just (a week) two days before I left Germany I heard bad news. I had just met a boy from Waskom and we were sitting on a stone watering-trough in Berncastel talking when another man came up. He and I had taken teacher's examinations together at Marshall six years ago. He said that he had just received a letter telling of the death of a mutual young lady friend. She had died of influenza, or at least of pneumonia following "flu." I shall tell you more about her some day. She was a splendid young woman, and I was very sorry to hear of her death.

. . .

Believe me, I had no intention of writing such a letter when I started. This is probably my last letter from Europe. Thanks be that it is. With all my love, I am,

Devotedly yours,

Eugene

P.S. There is some talk of the 360th parading in Houston. I hope it is rumor. I have not heard a man say that he wanted to parade. We all want to get out and get home.

Letter 40: June 9, 1919

My own dearest Myrtle,

You can not know how glad I am to be back once more in the U.S.A. I can't realize it fully yet myself. But that does not prevent me from knowing that I am really in that glorious land.

We landed in Boston Saturday just a little before noon. The voyage over took ten days and about ten or twelve hours. It seemed much longer than that. Quite a few of the boys got sick. Some of them even said they did not care if the boat should sink. We had some rough weather for about three days. Of course it was hardly a storm, but it was a close relation to one. I missed getting sick. Although I was dizzy several times.

Time passed slowly on the boat because we had nothing to do. I tried to read, but had only indifferent success. My mind has become quite unruly! I am afraid I wonder how hard it will be to get back to studying once more. We had shows, band concerts, services, etc. and they helped to pass the time. Also we had to stand about two hours each time in the chow line before we could get anything to eat. We ate only two meals a day. If we had had three, time would probably have passed faster, but most of us would have been fit subjects for the madhouse. I am so thoroughly disgusted with lining up that if anyone ever says anything to me about lining up, after I get out of the army, I am going to fight. The limit came yesterday morning when I had to get up, line up, and sign up a little card. Some other companies were going through the "delouser" (doesn't it sound terrible? I know no more empathetic term for the idea though, so you will have to pardon its use here on the ground of necessity) that same night. They have given us an enthusiastic welcome all along the line. We are now about forty miles from Boston. Every town that we passed through cheered and every locomotive and factory whistle was blowing. At least, it sounded that way. But this is perhaps not interesting, as you have read lots more about such things than I have seen here.

Chaplain Burns left this morning for Indiana to meet his wife and children at Indianapolis. He lives near Indianapolis. He was certainly a happy man. He has said all along that seeing his family was the best medicine they could give him. He will probably have to go to a tuberculosis hospital before he is discharged. He has a furlough for two weeks.

We don't know when we leave here. We may pull out tomorrow. That is the general opinion. You of course know that we are to spend one day in Houston and show ourselves off. I am glad the parade will last only about twenty minutes. It would have suited me all right to have gone straight on to Travis. However, it will take only one day longer. We are to be free all of our stay in Houston except for the marching time. I am glad of that, although I hardly know what I shall do, as I know very few people there, and those few not at all intimately enough to force myself upon them. I shall call you up that afternoon, after you get home from school. I don't suppose you are planning to come to Houston. It is only a short time, and there will be a big crowd there all day. I would run down to Edna if there was any chance to stay a few hours, but there is no way of doing that. I am getting mighty anxious to see you. I'll be thinking of you. You will be holding examinations I suppose. Wouldn't you like some help grading those examination papers? My willingness would be exceeded only by my ignorance.

The trip to Texas will probably take six days, maybe not more than five. If you should by any means be in Houston, be sure to let me know. All my time would be happily taken, if you should be there. I shall be in Headquarters Co. If any of the Arthurs come, tell them to be sure to look me up. I believe they would anyway, but I'll give them a special invitation to do so. I am not urging you to come, anxious as I am to see you. It will be for only a short time and there will be big crowds in from other towns. But if you are there, you must be sure to telegraph me just a short time before the train pulls in.

I can hardly realize, Myrtle, that in less than a month perhaps I shall be with you. It seems so far off even yet. But a month will soon pass.

My thoughts are always turning to you, my darling, and all my heart is yours.

Your own,

Eugene
Camp Devens, Massachusetts

Eugene and Myrtle married on March 2, 1922, and
shared a life together for the next 51 years.

Names in the Diary

Reese, Chaplain, Ist LT Clarence H.- Div HQ

Clark——3 or more possibilities

'Quarrels': Quarles, Cromwell B. Corporal

Chatfield, Lt. Lyman G, CAPT 9/17/18

Etter, Hall, Cpt., Major, May 15, 1918, Commanding 2nd Bat.

Morris, William H.H., Major, Commanding 1st Bat.

Hirsch, Cpl

Finkleburg, Morris, Lt. MD, killed September 14, 360th Inf

Newman, Simeon Harrison, Dr., 1st LT, Med Corp

Arthur, John, Machine Gun Co.

Crawford, Milton

'Ruder': Rueter, Henry, killed September 15

Hartell. Lt. Bn Adj

Givas, Jimmy, killed Sept 15, buried by McL

King, Roy R. Cpl, 315th F.S. Btn, killed September 15, buried by McL

'Braschol': Bratcher, Clarence E. killed September 20, buried by McL

Long, Jessie J, killed September 19, buried by McL

'Filligen': Fillingim, Marshall B., buried by McL

Karbowski, Otto H., Sgt, wounded Septmber 17 and died, buried by McL September 19

Irwin, Hal E., Sgt., killed September 14 buried by YMCA man

Spath, Cpl, killed by shellfire, buried by McL September 20

Holland, Fate W., buried by McL September 20

Bishop, Joe A., Sgt

Isaacks, John J., Co D runner

Watts, Will, Co D runner

Lewis, Walter O., 1st LT, Chaplain, 360 Inf.

Price, Howard C., Col, Commanding 360 Inf.

McDowell, Mr. of Boston

'Gunstreer': Gunstream, Walter L., Sgt. of the Scouts

Joiner, Lemuel L., a runner, wounded

Drohan, Lawrence P., Co. D, 360 Inf., killed October 5

Conley, Eugene J., Co D, 360 Inf. Killed October 5, McL buried him October 6

Little, Btn runner, wounded, shell shock, October 3

Hogg, Mike, Capt, Co. D, 360 Inf.

Nichols

Joiner, Arthur E., DSC, from Granbury Texas

Bond, William, Cpl (later Sgt)

Moreland, Sgt

Meeks, Gerald

Hirsch, Glenn

Ettor, Major, 2nd Btn

Boyd, John, of Lavaca, Texas

Wynne, Buck J, Lt

Maxwell, Cap, HQ Co

Kennedy, Sgt HQ Co

Thompson, William B., Cpt. Machine Gun Co, 360 Inf

Nelson, Ray, litter bearer 358 Field Hosp.

Hooper, Co D, wounded, from Brownwood, Texas

Delario, Charles E.,Cpt, killed November 2, Co A, 360 Inf., from Los Angeles

Bartlett, Lt

Lambertson, Tom, killed November1, 1918

Barden, Charlie, killed November 4, Father a Methodist minister near Goliad, Texas

Arthur, John, Machine Gun Co

**The grave in Elysian Fields, Texas, of Eugene William McLaurin
and Myrtle Alice Arthur McLaurin**

AN APPRECIATION

Below the Herald publishes an article from the pen of Rev. C. H. Reese, formerly pastor of the Victoria and Edna Episcopal churches, but recently senior chaplain in the 90th division. The article was addressed to the officers of the Edna Presbyterian Church and comes as an unsolicited but highly appreciated tribute to the gallant service rendered by E. W. McLaurin, pastor of the Edna Presbyterian Church, as the war just closed.

Houston, Texas

June 10, 1919

A statement concerning Rev. E. W. McLaurin,
Acting Chaplain 360th Infantry.

On September 12, 1918, Bishop Charles H. Brent, who was in charge of all chaplains of the American Expeditionary Forces, came to Villers en Haye France, the headquarters of the Ninetieth Division, and in the presence of Major General Henry T. Allen and his staff and Rev. Clarence H. Reese, who had just been appointed senior chaplain of the Ninetieth Division, suggested that if there was any clergyman in the ranks of the Ninetieth who would make a good chaplain, he be detailed as Acting Chaplain until such a time as a commission could be issued to him.

The same afternoon Chaplain Reese went to the 315 Supply Trains and got Rev. E. W. McLaurin and took him in a side car motorcycle to the 360 Infantry and he went over the top with the men of the 360th the next morning. The third day of the fight a shell exploded beside the Acting Chaplain McLaurin and for several days he was mentally unbalanced. He refused to be sent to the rear, however, and in less than a week recovered his poise and went on with the burial of the dead so energetically that the dead of the 360th Infantry were interred and its area cleared of dead bodies as quickly as any other.

On September 29th, Rev. Mr. McLaurin [prepared and submitted his application for a commission] exactly in accordance with instructions which he had received from Bishop Brent.

In the battle of the Meuse-Argonne Mr. McLaurin conducted himself with the greatest gallantry and in cooperation with Chaplain Walter O. Lewis buried over two hundred 360th Infantry dead, about one hundred and fifty dead of other American Divisions and nearly two hundred German Dead.

On the morning of the armistice – November 11, 1918 – the Adjutant of the Ninetieth Division, Major Owen J. Watts, received back from G. H. Q. the application of Acting Chaplain McLaurin for a commission with the statement that the regulations required one more endorsement. The Adjutant secured one more endorsement and had the papers on their way back to G. H. Q. before eleven o'clock, the hour when the armistice went into effect.

When the Division reached Germany the Adjutant was informed that no commissions (sic) could be issued to Mr. McLaurin because no more chaplains were being commissioned. The Assistant Chief of Staff and G-1 Col. E. V. D. Murphy took the matter up personally with G. H. Q. but was unable to accomplish anything. The Division Captain wrote several personal letters to Bishop Brent urging that vigorous action be taken to have a commission issued to Mr. McLaurin. The regiment is now about to be demobilized and still Rev. Mr. McLaurin is a private.

Mr. McLaurin is not protesting as he says it was a privilege to serve in any capacity, but his comrades, officers as well as enlisted men, without a known exception, feel that it was unjust to make a private do the work of an officer for several months with only the rank and pay of a private, and they desire very strongly that a commission be issued to Rev. Eugene

W. McLaurin and that he be given the pay of a chaplain for the period that he so splendidly performed the work of a chaplain, even though it may require a special act of Congress to accomplish this end.

Col. Howard C. Price, 360th Regiment, who signed the first endorsement to Mr. McLaurin's application, will corroborate the above statements.

Clarence H. Reese
Senior Chaplain, 90th Division